By the same author

A BISHOP AT PRAYER (SPCK)
THE ACTS THROUGH MODERN EYES (MOWBRAYS)
A BISHOP ON SAFARI (SPCK)

Leslie E. Stradling

Praying the Psalms

London SPCK

First published 1977
SPCK
Holy Trinity Church
Marylebone Road
London NW1 4DU

Printed in Great Britain by
Bocardo and Church Army Press
Cowley, Oxford

ISBN 0 281 02960 1

CONTENTS

ACKNOWLEDGEMENTS

The Book of Common Prayer 1662 is Crown copyright; extracts used herein are by permission.

Extracts from the Jerusalem Bible, published and © 1966, 1967, and 1968 by Darton, Longman & Todd Ltd and Doubleday & Co. Inc., are used by permission of the publishers.

Extracts from the New English Bible, second edition © 1970, are used by permission of Oxford and Cambridge University Presses.

Biblical quotations from the Revised Standard Version of the Bible, copyrighted 1946, 1952, © 1971, 1973 by the Division of Christian Education of the National Council of the Churches of Christ in the USA, are used by permission.

Thanks are due to Wm Collins Sons & Co. Ltd for permission to quote copyright material from *Reflections on the Psalms* by C. S. Lewis, and to Charlotte Baker Montgomery for permission to reproduce 'Pronouns' from *Dreamers on Horseback* by Karle Wilson Baker, published by the Southwest Press.

Introducing the Psalms

The prayer book instructs Anglican ministers 'to say daily Morning and Evening Prayer, either publicly or privately, not being hindered by sickness or some other urgent cause'. From the day of my ordination I accepted that obligation without question, and this means that, for most of my life, I have said at least two psalms and generally more every day.

In recent years the obligation has been widely questioned and many priests now say that they cannot in conscience be bound by what seems to them a formal and repetitive practice. Jesus warned us of the danger of offering to God words that are empty of meaning – even the Lord's prayer can be used in this way – and I am aware that I have often recited the words of the office without thinking. Yet over the years I have become deeply attached to these services, and particularly to the psalms which are an essential part of them, and I have no wish to break loose from them now.

In my love for the psalms I am following a tradition which has its roots in Christian history. John Chrysostom, for example, says that many of his contemporaries in the fourth century knew the whole psalter by heart and that such knowledge was often a prerequisite for ordination. His friend Palladius describes a forty-mile journey across the desert with a saint called improbably Heron, who neither ate nor drank all day but spent the time in reciting by heart fifteen psalms, then the 'long psalm', the Epistle to the Hebrews, the Gospel of Luke, and finally the Book of Proverbs. All this while he walked so fast that the others could scarcely keep up with him.

In monasteries the whole psalter has been recited weekly and a good deal of it daily. Patrick said all 150 psalms every day. In the seventeenth century Nicholas Ferrar gave up brilliant political prospects to join his brother and brother-in-law with their families in founding at Little

Gidding a community of prayer and work. They had a Sunday school which was so psalter orientated that its members were known as the psalm children. A prize of one penny, a considerable sum at that time, was given for every psalm learned by heart. They also had a watch each night during which the psalter was said straight through antiphonally. In more recent times Bonhoeffer at Finkenwalde used to pray the psalter through because it was for him 'the great school of prayer'.

A few years ago I woke up to the fact that this tradition was beginning to fade. It was being said that the psalms were on the way out, and some thought that they had gone for ever except as a fringe devotion. Few Anglicans in urban areas come to Matins now or even to Evensong, and when they do come they are likely to find only one psalm, and that one chosen because it is the shortest of those appointed. Except in religious houses, in some new eucharistic liturgies, and by those clergy who still say the daily office, the psalms are not much used today.

This state of affairs distressed me and I began wondering what could be done about it. No doubt one of the reasons for the lost appeal is the establishment of the hymnbook in the affection of worshippers, but how were we to persuade people that this comparatively modern development is welcome only when it supplements rather than displaces the psalter? The clergy might, for instance, teach their congregations about the psalms, or introduce the psalm appointed in the same way as a lesson is often introduced. As the psalms are a common heritage of all churches, we could use them widely in ecumenical worship.

Perhaps greater wisdom could be shown in deciding which psalms to choose for our services. In early days they were recited selectively, as they are to this day in the Roman breviary. To say them straight through from 1 to 150 was one of Cranmer's least happy innovations. It is like reading the Bible from the first chapter of Genesis steadily onwards. In fact it is so disastrous that I have wondered whether Cranmer had any real interest in the psalms. Contemporary lectionaries have wisely returned to the principle of selection. Moreover, the fact that they appoint fewer psalms for each service enables some people at least to say them more meaningfully.

Bible study groups could be encouraged to take a look at the psalms. I have not heard of one that did so. Here Hargreaves[1] would be particularly helpful with his four questions about each psalm: What is the experience behind it? In what way did God intervene? What is the psalmist's response to God? And how can I identify myself with each of these three stages?

Again we might consider those psalms which have been paraphrased into hymns and see if young writers and composers could be found who would do this in a contemporary idiom, thus compiling a new Scottish psalter for ecumenical use. *Psalm Praise* is a courageous attempt to do this. We might also examine critically our way of singing the psalms. Some like plainsong and some like Anglican chants but what attracts the average congregation is a tune of the Crimond sort. And when we say the psalms, should we say them in unison, or by the comparatively modern method of antiphonal verse recitation or by the more ancient method of saying half-verses antiphonally?

A fresh approach certainly seems to be needed. We could use a new translation. We could omit the duplicates (14, 18, 70, 108, 144). We could delete what is unintelligible or theologically unsound. (The new Roman breviary leaves out 58, 83, and 109 as 'they do not easily lend themselves to Christian usage'.) We could write brief introductions to each psalm. We could regroup them, as a hymnbook does, under such headings as praise and penitence. The difficulty would be, however, to reach any general agreement on what changes to make.

[1] See the bibliography at the end of this book.

For selection can be dangerous. In his *Global Odyssey* Howard Johnson wrote of Arab Anglicans in the Middle East:

> Some considerations gave me pause. One is the draft I was shown of a proposed new prayer book . . . I noticed first that the one hundred and fifty psalms of David has been reduced in number to one hundred. I have no quarrel with that *per se*. In public worship fifty of them might well go out. But by what criterion did some go out and some stay in? I was not long in discovering. Deleted was every psalm mentioning Israel!

It was as I pondered possible ways of rehabilitating the psalms that I realized how superficial had been my own study of them. Of course I had gone through them at my theological college, and there was a commentary or two – not very up to date – on my shelves, but my regular Bible study down the years had been based on the New Testament and especially on the Gospels. So I started to study them again, primarily to discover whether an interpretation of the text would help me to use the psalms better in public worship. The mystical and allegorical explanations which luxuriated in the Middle Ages had little appeal for me, but I wanted to know what I was doing when I regularly recited a verse so incomprehensible as: 'Though ye have lien among the pots, yet shall ye be like the wings of a dove that is covered with silver wings and her feathers like gold'. I wondered if we needed a new translation for use in church, and I found in the Jerusalem Bible edition 'for reading and recitation' an attempt to supply this need which did not quite come off.

It did not take me long to discover that, though there are some excellent commentaries,[1] many of the books on the psalms are geared to the scholar rather than to the general reader. Such questions as: Did David write this

[1] See the bibliography at the end of this book.

psalm? If he didn't who did? To what type does it belong? What is its poetic structure? How is it related to the Covenant festival? How was it sung in the temple? – may or may not interest us, but they do not help many people to pray the psalms. When the Epistle to the Hebrews ascribes Psalm 95 to David who certainly did not write it, does this concern us now?

Too many commentaries are mainly taken up with such questions. Thus the reviewer in *Theology* of Anderson's expensive two-volume commentary in the New Century Bible says: 'arriving at negative conclusions seems to take up a good deal of space. Considerable space is also occupied in looking at possible emendations of the text – again without much to show for it. He does not offer much help to anyone who reads the psalms in the RSV and wants to understand them.' Mitchell Dahood's three-volume commentary in the otherwise admirable Anchor Bible is almost completely unintelligible to a layman. Impatience with this sort of book tempts me to bypass the scholars, but this would be a serious mistake. What I have to do is to learn from them what I can and then go on to let their teaching guide me in my prayers; just as a motorist needs from time to time to go off the bypass into the towns in order to stock up with essential commodities before proceeding on his journey.

Gradually I discovered, or perhaps I rediscovered, the other tradition of individual meditation on the psalms. Jesus himself must have done this, for he used 22 and 31 at Calvary, quoted 110, 118, and 41 in his teaching – and surely what he said about himself as the good shepherd must have been partly derived from 23 – as well as singing the Hallel (113–18) in the upper room and speaking on the road to Emmaus of 'all that was written of me in the psalms'.

Christians have always interpreted the psalms in the light of their own beliefs and have tried to hear in them the voice of Christ. Sometimes it is quite impossible to do this and at other times we can do it only if we read into them all kinds of thoughts that were not in the mind of the original composers. Thus the military references to Israel's wars with their neighbours have to be applied to wars on the frontiers of faith; the occasional hints of a life after death have to be read in the light of resurrection glory.

The apostles used the psalms in their teaching about Christ, and I cannot see how they could have done this unless they had meditated long upon them in their own prayers. Peter at Pentecost quoted extensively from 16 which he misunderstood and misinterpreted, as we are all liable to do though not always with such happy results as he achieved. Paul quoted 2 in the synagogue at Pisidian Antioch, 68 in writing to the Ephesian church – the famous phrase about 'leading captivity captive' – and he and Silas sang psalms in the prison at Philippi.

Rowland Prothero's *The Psalms in human life* – first published in 1903 – quotes a vast number of instances to show what the psalms have meant to famous men and women down the years and all over the world. Athanasius spoke for the early Church when he compared the psalter to a garden where, because every variety of prayer grows all the year round, we can go in at any time and pick freely. Luther's love of the psalms is shown in the lectures on them with which he began his career as a teacher, in his psalm-based hymns, and in his affection for the 'old and ragged' psalter which went everywhere with him. In the last century Perowne spoke for more modern times: 'No single book of scripture . . . unless it be the gospels, has had so large an influence in moulding the affections, sustaining the hopes, and purifying the faith of believers.'

It soon became obvious to me that I too could be helped by meditating on the psalms in my personal prayers. But first some difficulties had to be overcome because I found that I could not get far without being critical of certain aspects of the psalter.

What was I to make of the many ugly and cursing passages? 58 appears to contain no spiritual message at all. 137 which begins so beautifully ends with: 'Blessed shall he be that taketh thy children and throweth them against the stones.' I have heard a South African priest plead for the retention of these verses on the ground that this is an effective way of praying for his government. Gelineau defends them by applying them to the forces of evil since, he maintains, 'if we are incapable of hatred we are incapable of love'. The New Testament writers are not squeamish about the curses either, but appear to quote them with relish. But perhaps it is because there are so many cursing passages and so much violence in the press and on TV that we do not find them congenial when they intrude into our prayers.

Nor can I feel at home with some of the theology in the psalter. It is, for instance, taken for granted that the righteous are rewarded and the wicked punished in this life, just as if we were living in a traditional 'western' novel where the villain is always disposed of and the hero always triumphs. It is assumed that the heavens declare the glory of God, whereas to many moderns all that they declare is the impersonal immensity of the universe. It is taken for granted that God's hand is visible in history, but nowadays it often seems as if God is on holiday. It is accepted without question that the universe is a three-storeyed structure. Forgiveness is supposed to include the remission of any penalty. The psalmist's attitude to sickness and suffering is open to many understandings.

For the purpose of my own prayers I simply ignored all those verses which I found unacceptable as they stood or incapable of honest reinterpretation. We cannot, however, easily do this in our public worship, and so it looks as if some process of selection is essential.

In my meditations I use Miles Coverdale's translation as it is found in the Anglican prayer book, and in my commentary I have used the psalm numbering and the verse numbering of that book. This is because it is the version with which I am most familiar and which I dearly love, but each reader of the psalms should shop around until he finds a version with which he can feel happy. I have kept detailed references to a minimum, and anyone who uses a modern translation – such as RSV from which most of my other biblical quotations come – should have little difficulty in following me.

It may be asked on what principle I have chosen these twenty-six psalms for comment. I suppose it was because they had something to say to me at particular moments of my life, and I hope that my readers will go direct to the psalter and find help in many other psalms. But anyone who is going to do this must make himself sufficiently familiar with the psalter to know which psalm to turn to in case of need. Nicholas Ferrar could tell you immediately what psalm to use when you were ill or bereaved or frustrated or happy or grateful, but it seems that most people now can remember only 23, and presumably that is the reason why it is used indiscriminately for all occasions including funerals and weddings. Some psalms did not appeal to me because I found them noisy and full of shouting when what I needed was quiet. Some made their point by hammering me when what I needed was reason. We all have to discover what psalms were written specially for us.

When we have found our way around – and there is less continuity in the psalter than there is in a hymnbook – we could sometimes, instead of dwelling on one psalm as a unity, pull out individual verses and rest in them. Like Shakespeare, the psalter is full of quotations, and we could make our own treasury of them. What I have occasionally done is to take a theme, such as trust, and follow this through the psalter, thus building up a sort of canticle about it. The South African prayer book has an example of this in its 'Commendation of the soul'.

Whatever happens, we must not lose one of the greatest treasures of our devotional heritage. So I invite you to seek the guidance of the Holy Spirit and to join me in praying the psalms and in listening to what God has to say to us through them.

Prayers of Praise

1 O COME, LET US SING (95)

This psalm speaks to us about the power of God, who is a great king above all gods and the strength of our salvation. He is the almighty one which does not mean that he can do anything, for there are some things which he cannot do; he cannot act in a way contrary to his own nature, as he would be doing if, for instance, he told a lie. The word 'almighty' means that God is the source of all power, the ruler of the universe and the lord of all.

The power of God is seen first in the world at large and in the things that happen. The prophets – especially Amos, Isaiah, and Jeremiah – taught us that history is controlled by God from beginning to end. For them, God dominates the nations, guiding them, imposing his will upon them, punishing them. The psalm endorses this view when it says: 'In his hand are all the corners of the earth.' Anything that goes on in any place and at any time is directed by him, and he is the origin of whatever strength there is anywhere. Often it is impossible for us to understand this, for the nations seem to laugh at God's orders and to get on with their life in their own way. Modern young people ask whether God can 'interfere' without making a nonsense of all the laws he has laid down for the ordering of the world. And if he could do so, why doesn't he? Faith is called for here, faith to believe that God is in command, whatever the appearances to the contrary may be.

God's power in the world is seen in his maintenance of order. He created order out of chaos, and he sees to it that chaos will never return. This is also the function of human administration, for there would be no point in having a government if all the citizens knew how to live happily together without one; or in having policemen if no laws were ever broken; or in having doctors if no one ever fell ill or died; or in having maintenance engineers if all machines serviced themselves. So when we assert our belief that we have a sovereign God we are also proclaiming that his creation needs to be preserved. The Lord is our maker who is also our sustainer. He is a great king above all gods, among whom are included those earthly rulers who have made themselves into gods.

God's power in the world is also shown by the fact that history is working towards a final purpose. This is the end which drew near when Christ came but which has not yet reached its fulfilment. Christ is the one who has come, but he is also to come. History is not a meaningless collection of events, going round in circles as is suggested by the last verse of the hymn 'It came upon the midnight clear'. We believe that at the end of the day God will bring his purpose to a triumphant conclusion. The Lord *is* a great God.

Our response to God's power in the world should be that of faith. We say Yes to him, for his arm is powerful and he is our shield and our rock. We believe in his power – and may he help our unbelief.

The power of God is seen secondly in salvation, for 'he is the strength of our salvation', mighty to save. He is the God of hosts, the lord of the heavenly armies. He made us, called us to be his children, sent his Son to die for us, showed his power above all in the resurrection and new creation. He never makes mistakes and he always keeps his promises to us who are 'the people of his pasture and the sheep of his hand'.

Once I saw in the Anglican Cathedral at Johannesburg a large notice headed: 'This is power'. Underneath was a list of the Eucharists for the coming week, with a space for people to write their initials in order to signify which service they would attend. For the power of the resurrection life flows through this sacrament, and those who wrote their initials proclaimed and praised this power. In most of the new liturgies, when the priest says at the time of communion: 'The body of Christ', the communicant replies: 'Amen', thereby asserting that he is receiving more than a wafer which might remind him of Christ. He is receiving the power of Christ himself.

Besides the Eucharist, God sends us his power through the scriptures, through preaching, through prayer, and through sharing in Christian fellowship. Once we have begun to know what the power of God in salvation means, we shall want to 'rejoice heartily in the Lord, and come before his presence with thanksgiving'.

The power of God is seen thirdly in suffering love. It is not that his power can be seen in spite of all the evil and the failure, but that it can be seen precisely *in* suffering love.

For halfway through this psalm its mood changes. The joyful music suddenly ends and there is heard a prophetic voice giving an austere warning. We are told that the praise of God cannot be separated from a readiness to hear his voice – Christ's sheep hear his voice! – and to obey him. 'Those who sing gospel psalms', says Matthew Henry, 'must live gospel lives.' If we call Jesus master and lord, we must do what he says. The inner truthfulness of the heart is supremely important.

The glorious exodus from Egypt was followed by the disgraceful incidents at Meribah ('Provocation') and at Massah ('Temptation'), where there was quarrelling, fault-finding, and a general falling away from faith as the people tried to make God serve their own ends. At Massah they asked: 'Is the Lord among us or not?' – and John was later to show that unbelief is the root sin. When we slam the door in God's face, there comes the inevitable hardening of our heart, so that it becomes a rock on which the falling seed can bear no fruit.

But to my mind the most striking verse is: 'Forty years long was I grieved with this generation'. The almighty lord of creation and history and salvation is grieved – he suffers – because of the misbehaviour of an insignificant and tiresome tribe of nomads. The almighty God seems strangely weak and vulnerable here, and yet the power of his love is seen especially in this weakness.

We say in the words of the Sanctus: 'Holy, holy, holy Lord God of hosts; heaven and earth are full of your glory.' As far as heaven is concerned, it is not hard to imagine that as being full of the power and the glory of God. But what do we mean when we say with Isaiah that the whole *earth* is full of God's power and glory? The press tells us that the earth is full of injustice, erosion, poverty, terrorism, unemployment, disease, illiteracy, drought, pollution, war. I take Isaiah to mean, not that every single aspect of earthly life is packed with God's glory, but that the glory is to be seen if we look for it. When someone says 'Chicago is full of gangsters', he does not mean that every single person in Chicago is a gangster, but that there are a number of such people in that city, and that if you go looking for them you are likely to find them. So God's power and glory can sometimes be seen clearly against a background of darkness. We can see it, for instance, in the rapt dedication of worshippers in a slum church, or in those who are ready to forgive and to work for reconciliation when a parish is divided into factions. We can see it too in the first Eastertide when Jesus appeared to the travellers on the Emmaus road, whom he himself called dull, blind fools.

The prayer book collect for Trinity XI begins: 'O God, who declarest thy almighty power *most chiefly in* showing mercy and pity . . .' The power is shown especially in his forgiveness and compassion towards those who are weak. At a weekday service in a London church the dozen people present all struck me as being odd. There was a girl who was sobbing most of the time and, in the intervals of doing so, was jotting down notes on an already overcrowded piece of paper. There was a young man who dragged a heavy suitcase about from pew to pew, and an old man with the biggest ear-trumpet I have ever seen. There was the clergyman with hair cascading down over his shoulders, and there was an old woman who was tied up with string. Had I been paying attention to my prayers I should not have noticed any of these things, but as it was I began to think that I was the only normal person in the church. But then God put into my mind these words of Paul:

> Consider your call, brethren; not many of you were wise according to worldly standards, not many were powerful, not many were of noble birth; but God chose what is foolish in the world to shame the wise, God chose what is weak in the world to shame the strong, God chose what is low and despised in the world (1 Cor. 1. 26-8).

Then I realized that it was I who was the odd man out, and that these others – the foolish, the weak, the despised – were the true Christian norm. The Lord saw that they needed him, and so he showed the power of his love by calling them to himself. Divine love may suffer apparent defeats from time to time, but in the end it is victorious, and this is what we mean when we proclaim that God is almighty. And this is the lesson we have to learn here – to be, not only workers, but lovers, together with God.

If we are going to do this, we must also notice that this psalm goes on to say: 'Today if you will hear his voice harden not your hearts.' The ancient theatre at Epidaurus in Greece, seating 15,000 people, is still used and its acoustics cannot be faulted. A whisper, the crushing of a piece of paper, the striking of a match, can be clearly heard even on the back row. Yet when I was there, some tired children were running about, shouting and crying, and then it became impossible to pick up anything more than the louder sounds.

In the stillness of the desert the Israelites should have

found conditions ideal for listening to God's voice, but instead they allowed themselves to be distracted by the noise of other voices and by their own inattention. The strain on the covenant relationship was great there, for God was grieved with them for forty years. A woman said to me: 'I loathe and hate my husband, but what can I do? I am a Christian, so I must stay with him for as long as he wants me?' Many would question whether she was right to stay with him if it was true that her love was dead but, however that may be, we can only be grateful that God goes on loving us even after our love for him has died. There is a danger that we should grieve God continually by our rebellious and revolutionary behaviour and by our efforts to overthrow his government in our lives. 'Today if you will hear his voice', therefore, 'harden not your hearts.'

On the first Easter evening in the upper room at Jerusalem the congregation was pathetic. Nowadays we are accustomed to small numbers on Sunday evening, but here there were only ten people in church, including the bishop who was to preach. The atmosphere was defeatist: perhaps because of recent press criticism. The sermon was competent but it was about religious doubt and it lacked punch. Then suddenly Jesus stood among them, almighty, full of power. He preached on belief, filled them with his Spirit, gave them his peace, ate with them, made them glad, and sent them out together to change the world.

2 CORPORATE THANKSGIVING (107)

In this psalm four groups of people come to the temple to give thanks in four stanzas of the same pattern, each with the double refrain:

> They cried unto the Lord in their trouble,
> And he delivered them from their distress.
> O that men would therefore praise the Lord for his goodness,
> And declare the wonders that he doeth for the children of men.

The first group consists of travellers safely home after an arduous journey, the second of prisoners released from gaol, the third of sick who have recovered, and the fourth of seafarers who have survived a dangerous voyage. The shape of the psalm reminds us of the eucharistic thanksgiving with its proper prefaces. There may have been an annual thankday in the temple, for which people saved up the expression of their gratitude. Today in church we hear groups of people publicly prayed for, but rarely see them offering public thanks for prayer that has been answered.

The psalm does not claim that all who pray to the Lord in their trouble will be delivered by him from their distress. In the final section (where the style changes to that of a choir hymn in the Wisdom style, cool and impersonal, with the human interest lost in generalized statements on divine providence) it is openly accepted that God does not guarantee that things will always happen as we should like. He 'turns the floods into a wilderness, makes a fruitful land barren, permits us to be brought low by plague or evil intreated by tyrants, and lets us wander out of the way in the wilderness'.

Yet the main conviction of the psalm is that God can

and does transform the world. He can create a fertile land out of the Arabah or the Sahara, and he does this through the skills he gives for rural development. He feeds the starving and undernourished through programmes of Christian aid. He makes nations multiply exceedingly and then offers conception control to redress the balance. When we misuse the world's resources, creation goes bad on us, but we can expect a blessing when we share the good things that God gives us.

The opening three verses form a general introduction and set the theme, which is that God redeems us, delivers us, and gathers us together in his Church from the four corners of the earth. These verses are marvellously enriched when we interpret them in the light of Good Friday and Easter, and apply to them the prophecy of Caiaphas that 'Jesus should die for the nation, and not for the nation only, but to gather into one the children of God who are scattered abroad'.

The travellers in the first group thought it a miracle that they had got home safely. South Africa is familiar with these travellers' tales. When, for instance, the Grosvenor, an East Indiaman, was wrecked off the coast in 1782, the survivors made their way south through hostile and inhospitable country, and most of them died of hunger, exhaustion, or sickness, but in an epic of endurance a few got through, and presumably they 'praised the Lord for his goodness'. To put this section in modern terms, we should need to talk of escapes from hijackings, air crashes, death on the roads, kidnappings, and holdups. Even if we ourselves have had no dramatic escapes, we take our life in our hands every time we leave our own front door, and we should never become so accustomed to the risks of travel as to forget to thank God every time he brings us safely home again.

The next group are the prisoners who have come out of the darkness and gloom of an ancient, unlighted prison. This may set us thinking of all the prisoners for conscience sake from Jeremiah and Paul to Bonhoeffer, but the prisoners here are in fact not cases for Amnesty International since they have been put inside for rebellion against God's laws. Previously they did not ask for God's advice, either because they did not see how this could help them, or because they were too busy to ask him, but long hours of idleness in prison had driven them to prayer. Now they have been delivered, for God has broken the gates of brass, secured the remission of their sentence long before they had dared to hope for it, and brought them into freedom.

Even though we may have no experience of literally being in gaol, most of us spend a considerable time in prisons of our own making. We allow ourselves to be shut up in our self-centredness, worldliness, doubt, routine, or sin. We say that we can do nothing without God's help, but we scarcely believe that, and we go on doing our own thing, and God has to bring our hearts low and break our stubborn wills before he can bring us out of the darkness. It was one of the points contained in Christ's policy statement at Nazareth that he is willing to arrange our escape from prison at any time (Luke 4. 18-19).

The third group is made up of sick people. We have to deny, with Job, the implication here that all sickness is a punishment for sin, yet we cannot help wondering whether, if there were no sin in the world, there would be any sickness either, and whether this is the truth that lies behind the fog of Christian Science. But leaving aside the cause of sickness, we may know enough about recovery from serious illness, whether in ourselves or in others, to be able to apply this section to ourselves. God sent his word – his Word, Jesus – and showed us our weakness and the folly of thinking that we were strong and important. He said: Be clean! Be whole! and he healed us.

The last group are the seafarers. Addison praised this description of the storm as sublime poetry and, if we have experienced the terrors of a gale in a modern liner, we can imagine how much more alarming it must have been in a small wooden ship of ancient times. There is a proverb which says that a man had better not go to sea unless he can pray, and the number of lives lost each year in small vessels reminds us that man has not finally conquered the sea any more than he has finally conquered disease.

As we read this psalm, we can also hear the Lord praising his Father for his own deliverance. He stayed in the wilderness of temptation, far from a city, where he was hungry and thirsty and his soul fainted within him, but his Father delivered him, satisfied him, and filled him with goodness. At Golgotha he sat in darkness and in the shadow of death, his hands and his feet bound with the misery of iron nails, falling down perhaps on the Way of Sorrows with only a stranger to help him – and all this, not on account of his own wrongdoing, but because his brethren lightly regarded God's counsel. (His heart, however, was never brought down through heaviness or through anything else.) But his Father led him out of the darkness of the tomb, loosed him from his graveclothes, and raised him from the dead. As far as we know Jesus was never sick, but he sympathized profoundly with others in their illness, whether or not it was for their own offence that they were plagued. More than once he was at death's door, in his final passage through death he offered the perfect sacrifice, and he still tells out with gladness his Father's wonderful works. He knew also about going down to the sea in ships. On one occasion he slept through a storm when his friends thought that their last hour had come. During another storm he walked on the wild water, making the storm to cease and the waves to be still, and he brought them to the land to which they were going.

If the psalmist had been writing today,the groups that

he selected might have been different, but the cries of their distress would have had the same notes:

Some got into a tangle with their personal relationships,
There was misunderstanding and recrimination.
They differed from each other in attitudes and values
But were unable to be open about their differences,
So they were churned up in their hearts through their shortcomings,
Frustrated and depressed and wallowing in self-pity.
Then they cried to their saviour who had redeemed them by his passion,
And he delivered them from their distress.

Some walked in constant fear of failure,
Having been given tasks beyond their competence,
Walking a tightrope, receiving no encouragement,
Somehow carrying on though daily threatened with dismissal.
Then they cried to their saviour who had redeemed them by his passion,
And he taught them how to suffer nobly with him.

Some were overwhelmed by deep guilt feelings.
They desired a life of holiness but could not find it.
The burden of their sins pressed heavily upon them.
The most that they could hope for was a life of reparation.
Then they cried to their saviour who had redeemed them by his passion,
And he delivered them from their distress.

Others are despised because of their colour.
They resent the fact that many jobs are closed against them.
They are bitter because treated as less than human,
And rejected or ignored or made to look inferior,
Their human dignity diminished, their human rights infringed.

They hunger passionately for their freedom,
So they cry to their saviour who has redeemed
them by his passion,
But when will he deliver them from their distress?

There are those who were bereaved and stayed in darkness,
Living in the past since the present was empty for them,
Every new situation stirring up old memories,
Desiring only death that they might join the loved one.
Health suffered and friends could not help them.
Then they cried to their saviour who had redeemed
them by his passion,
And he entered into their distress and shared it with
them.

The world is like a traveller lost in the desert.
It is a prisoner, a sick man, a shipwrecked mariner,
With its segregation and dictatorships and communism,
Its violence and hatred and aggression.
But when it turns to the saviour who has redeemed
it by his passion,
Then he will deliver it from its distress and recreate it.

The church too has often wandered in the wilderness
of corruption,
A captive, imprisoned in its own tradition,
Sick with unbelief and legalistic structures,
Almost wrecked in storms of materialism and false
ideology.
Then we cried to God our saviour who had redeemed
us by his passion,
And he delivered us from our distress and renewed us.

In these, as in all other instances of deliverance, we too must conclude by saying: O that men would praise the Lord for his goodness – in reconciling brothers, in standing by us in our distress, in the assurance of forgiveness, in overcoming conflict, for comfort in bereavement, for his love for the world and the Church – and then go on to declare to others the wonders that God does for the children of men.

3 RECOLLECTION (139)

This is a psalm of praise to God, creator and heartsearcher, who continues to preserve us in spite of knowing all our secrets. Here is no philosophical treatise on God's omniscience, omnipotence, and omnificence, but a vivid and moving meditation on the mystery of God's presence with us. It demands from us not so much a commentary as a translation, using contemporary terms, into our own experience.

Lord, you have an enormous file on me. Your informers report all my movements, and you know what armchair, what theatre seat, what office stool I sit on, how I respond to my alarum clock and early cup of tea, the path I follow to factory, swimming pool, or church. You even have bugging devices to record my thoughts. You have photostats of all my air tickets, expense accounts, and hotel bookings. You have on tape everything I say in public and in private. You created me and you sustain me to the last detail.

Lord, I don't know how you do it. I am astounded by your incredibly detailed knowledge, and I cannot begin to compete with your efficiency. However unrecollected I may be about you – and I am often very unrecollected both in my prayers and outside them – you are always recollected about me. At first I found your knowledge of me to be paralysing rather than liberating. Your eye – you as the divine voyeur – terrified me. How dared I speak or act when the expert was watching me? So my first reaction was a desire to escape from this surveillance. Yet I knew that your 'wonderful and excellent' closeness to me was in my own best interests, and I came to thank you for it, and for the way in which it brings to fruition whatever good seeds you have planted in me.

In any case it is futile to want to escape, because I could not do that if I tried. If I climb up into heaven – in prayer, friendship, relaxation – you are there in love. When I am in the hell of sin and rebellion, in a place so unclean that I should not have expected to find you in it, you are there in judgement.[1] If I take the morning jet and fly to the most distant spot in the world, or to the frontiers of faith and suffering, you meet me there and hold me fast, for your love has no limits. When the night closes round me and the darkness steals over me – the darkness of criticism, failure, pain, and death – that darkness will become as bright as day, because darkness and light are both under your control, and you are the light of the world. Realizing your closeness to me I turn to you, in penitence certainly, but also in trust.

Your care for me is shown by my creation, for which you were personally responsible, by the miracle of my existence which began when I was conceived in your thought aeons before I was conceived in my mother's womb. Your counsels – your thoughts – are precious to me, although often I do not understand them, for your thoughts, Divine Thinker, are higher than my thoughts. You would not have created me if you had not loved me – I know that I am not an unwanted child – and so I can approach you with confidence.

Lord, I hate evil because it is done before your eyes and it is offensive to you. I pray that evil may be overcome, and that I may take my share in overcoming it.[2] But I do not say this imagining that I am already perfect.

[1] The correct text reads: 'make my bed in hell' – surely an uncomfortable spot in which to spend even a night.

[2] But perhaps we should put verses 19-22 in brackets, for they are a sad lapse from the spiritual depth of the rest of the psalm. C. S. Lewis remarks on the naive way in which it is suggested to God that the simplest way for him to get rid of sin would be for him to kill all sinners. The psalmist finds it incredible that God lets the wicked continue in their wicked ways when he knows all the things that they are up to. But we can at least applaud the writer's burning indignation against injustice.

I know that there is evil in me too, and I am ready to face up to your audit, however painful that may be. If I am on the wrong lines, I trust that you will put me straight and renew me in such a way that I may find happiness in the integrity which you have given me.

Lord, above all lead me in the way that leads to eternal life.

4 WHAT IS MAN? (8)

This psalm begins and ends with adoration, with praise for the Lord our governor, our sovereign, whose excellence, majesty, glory, is shown by his control over nature, by his victory against his enemies, by his love for us (his 'mindfulness' which quietens our anxieties), by his direction of us (he 'visits' us and strengthens our will), and by the power which he has delegated to us. The emphatic 'thou' which opens the fifth and sixth verses makes it clear that it is God alone who gives us significance. We are to look beyond whatever power man may have to God who gave it to us and on whose behalf we exercise a measure of control over nature, and to whom we are answerable for what we do with that control, and in the singing of whose praises we are to break the heavenly sound barrier.

These ideas are beautifully expressed and they bring confidence and joy, but similar thoughts are frequent in the psalter. What is unusual, and very modern, is this psalmist's reflections on the greatness and the smallness of man, on his power and his weakness ('babes and sucklings'), and on his likeness to God.

What is man that thou are mindful of him? The true answer to this question is given by the writer to the Hebrews who, in commenting on this psalm, sees Christ entering into our humanity, waking it up out of its spiritual death, and taking it back home with him as his most precious possession.

When the gipsy tells your fortune, it is commonly believed that she looks at the lines in your left palm to see what you were intended to be, and then at those in your right palm to see whether you have done better or worse than that. So I look at my left hand and there I see a portrait of the saint that God meant me to be, and then I look at my right hand and see the spiritual disappointment that I have become. But to discover what I really am, I have to look away from both my hands, and even from my inmost heart, to God who has done great things for me. I tried to crown myself with glory and honour ('worship'), and was depressed by my complete inability to do so, and then quite unexpectedly God himself gave me the crown.

That is the Christian answer, but other answers have been given from time to time. What is man? The ancient Greeks said optimistically that he is the most significant and meaningful part of the universe. There are many wonders in the world, but none more wonderful than man. They looked into their left hand and equated potential with fact, so they gave 'glory to man in the highest, for man is the measure of things'. Hamlet agreed: 'What a piece of work is man! how noble in reason! how infinite in faculty! in form and moving how express and admirable! in action how like an angel! in apprehension how like a god! the beauty of the world!'

The modern westerner also agrees. Man is the scientist and the technocrat who harnesses nuclear power, travels to the moon, and controls disease. He has always had power over animals, birds, and fishes, but now there are no limits to his power. He is the centre of the universe and more successful than Adam in claiming equality with God. This would be a reasonable answer if we believed that there is no God.

What is man? Others give a pessimistic answer. Job asked the question, and in his bitterness replied: 'I am an insignificant nothing; why doesn't God let me alone? How can he possibly think that I am worth persecuting?' Another psalm asked the same question and came up with the answer that 'man is like a thing of nought: his time passeth away like a shadow'. Hamlet, too, after praising man to the skies, went on to describe him as 'the quintessence of dust'. When God has the heavens to look at, why should he want to look at us? (I admit that I have sometimes found it more satisfying to contemplate a landscape than a group of people, though even I have never gone as far as Ionides, the East African naturalist, who considered snakes to be less obnoxious than human beings.) According to this answer, man is no more than a cog in a machine, a speck of dust that feels dizzy as it looks up into space, a ghost in an animal body, a monkey who has come up in the world; and he is very far from being the centre of the universe.

Man is certainly powerful, but it looks as if he might be power-drunk, and all set to contaminate the earth for the powers of evil rather than to consecrate it for God. We live under the threat that we might see our planet totally destroyed, and this time there appears to be no Noah in sight, no ark and no rainbow. Power has gone bad on man, and the same things which lift him up also drag him down. Some moral standards have collapsed, and science has been unable to fill the gap which they have left; and it seems that after all the hymn is true when it says that 'every prospect pleases and only man is vile'. This too would be a reasonable answer if Christ had never risen and ascended.

What is man? What is this man? What am I? The answer does not depend on our own estimate of ourselves, but on what God thinks of us. And we know what that is when we recall how Christ, who really is at the centre of the universe, descended – condescended – to take our human nature, and to reveal himself through our human nature, and then he ascended, taking our human nature up with him into the heavenly sphere and giving us a share in his divine nature. At the ascension man was clothed with glory and honour because Christ, as the representative man, was then crowned with glory and honour. We have the glory, but it is not something that we have worked for; it is God's gift to us. If all things are in subjection to man, it is God who has made this possible. Our lives may seem finite and transient and sinful and sad, but in fact they are nothing of the sort, because Christ has made us equal to the angels, sons and daughters of God, children of the resurrection mature and responsible persons made in God's image so that we can know and love and serve him. Christ is renewing us and he is leading us into a glorious future.

5 ADORATION (19)

C. S. Lewis calls this 'the greatest poem in the psalter and one of the greatest lyrics in the world'. In it two separate psalms have been put together. The first six verses speak of the glory of God in nature, and remind us of Psalm 8, but the remaining verses are in a different metre, as the Jerusalem Bible makes clear, and they speak of the glory of God in the law, and remind us of Psalm 119. The link between the two parts is praise for God's glory and for his almighty presence in both nature and grace. In this sunrise hymn the heavens declare the creative power of God, and the gospel declares his power in his new creation. This is presumably what Kant meant when he said that the sky above us and the moral law within us witness to the same God. God's skies with their silent voices preach the creator of all races, and his Word preaches similarly the redemption of all men. It is appropriate that this psalm should be used on Christmas Day since what God showed us of himself in the world and in the law was the perfect preparation for what he showed us when he became man.

The first part of the psalm was paraphrased by Joseph Addison (it appears in English Hymnal 297, where no credit at all is given to the original writer!) and it forms a morning hymn which can be used on any day of the year:

The spacious firmament on high,
With all the blue ethereal sky,
And spangled heavens, a shining frame,
Their great Original proclaim.
The unwearied sun from day to day
Does his Creator's power display,
And publishes to every land
The works of an almighty hand.

The heavens declare the glory of God. The picture is of a solid vault or dome, upholding the celestial swimming pool out of which the plug could be pulled when rain was wanted on the earth. Primitive people could construct a theory about how the rain works and how the stars move, and they could wonder at this. How much more should we with our greater knowledge of space and astronomy be filled with wonder?

The heavens declare God's glory, but in our thoughts we can extend this to all the works of nature. I picture in my mind the river Vaal at a point where the banks are thickly wooded, with weeping willows at the edge, then poplars irregularly ranked and now bare of leaves, and darker bluegums behind. The river itself is 'a sea of glass like unto crystal', and the trees are reflected in it with startling clarity except where a mist rises to obscure them. Also upward rising, as if in praise, is the frozen breath of a labourer and the smoke of a bonfire.

Nature is not only glorious, says the psalmist, it is perfect, and day and night following each other in uninterrupted order testify to this perfection. It never goes wrong, as Nomgause the Xhosa prophetess expected that it would when she foretold that the sun would rise in the west one day in 1834, thus almost causing the suicide of her nation. This order in the universe was praised by Job when he spoke of the morning stars singing together and the sons of God shouting for joy.

The reference to the sun is based on an ancient eastern legend whose theme appeared also in the story of Helios the Greek god of the sun. The sun is a joyful giant, running his course, sleeping in the arms of his bride under the waters in which he finishes his day's work, and then returning by a short cut through the underworld to start the next day again. The sun is perfect, true, pure, and all the other things that are to be said later in the psalm about the law. But as it is possible to hide from the sun's heat, and more so than ever in these days of airconditioning, so it is possible to hide from the heat of God's love, and more so than ever in these days of technological self-sufficiency.

We join the psalmist as he contemplates with adoration the majesty of God in creation. Whether or not we share his rapture, we kneel in awe before the infinite wisdom and power and goodness of the eternal mind; and we see in nature, not only a collection of matter living and dead, of laws and formulas, but a revelation which points to Jesus who is the source of all light, and to the apostles and gospel preachers who are the stars.

The second part of the psalm concerns the law of the Lord, which includes not only the ten commandments, but the prophetic teaching, and every revelation of God's will. The Christian interprets it in terms of grace, the gospel, the scriptures, and indeed of Christ himself.

First there are six beautifully balanced statements about the law of the Lord – and Christians could well say 'Jesus' instead of 'the Lord'. In each statement there is a different noun to indicate some aspect of the law, an adjective to describe that aspect, and then a description of its positive effect. Each modern translation has its own rendering and, by doing a sort of Gallup Poll, I get the following result:

The law of the Lord is perfect,
  new life for the soul.
The instruction of the Lord is trustworthy,
  wisdom even for the simple.
The precepts of the Lord are right,
  joy for the heart.
The commandments of the Lord are clear,
  light for the eyes.
The fear of the Lord is good,
  lasting for ever.

The judgements of the Lord are pure,
righteous every one.

Then the law is praised as being like gold and honey, and we are happy if, with the psalmist, we find in our own experience that the gospel is both precious and sweet. Here is that personal religion where commandments and duties are replaced by an encounter with the living God to whom we give ourselves in confident faith.

The psalm continues with a prayer for cleansing, for the gift of a clear conscience. It sees sin as ignorance and indeed there are many faults which are secret from us, but all too obvious to everyone else. Who can tell how (often) he offends? In order to assist our self-examination in these days when lists of sins are unfashionable, we could use the beatitudes, for example, as a yardstick. Norman Goodacre finds it helpful to base our inquiry on personal relationships – in the family, in our work, towards God. But the psalmist also sees sin as presumption, rebellion, defiance, which unless it is overcome by God's power gets out of hand and rules over us. It is good that the thought of penitence and of God's cleansing power should come in here, but it must be kept in its place and not allowed to interfere with the main theme of the psalm, which is adoration and praise.

Finally, in the last two verses there is a prayer for acceptance. The psalmist wants the meditation of his heart – a phrase which reveals his profound insight into prayer – to be always acceptable. We note the word 'always', because the meditations that we make before a crucifix may be more acceptable than those we make before a mirror; for we are in fact meditating all day long, whether or not we are conscious of God's presence. Normally in the Old Testament the word 'acceptable' refers to the right offering made in the temple, but here it describes the offering of our hearts. This is a notable advance, and yet it falls far short of the Christian understanding that it is only the sacrifice of Christ which makes acceptable anything that we may offer to God. He alone is our strength and our redeemer.

6 SORROW INTO JOY (30)

Sometimes when rewriting a psalm in Christian terms, I try to recapture, not its original rhythm, but something of its rhythmic feel. I have no illusions about producing great poetry in this way – though the poetry that is there keeps breaking through – but it helps me in my prayers. I give an example of this in the hope that it may encourage others to experiment along these lines.

Jesus I praise; he raised me up.
My foes attacked; he threw them down.
Jesus, Lord God, I cried to you;
In your great love you healed my soul.

My feet had slipped down towards hell.
Forgetting you, I trusted self.
You snatched me back, you kept me safe,
Your risen power gave me new life.

When you are close I stand secure.
Jesus, your love is rocklike, strong.
But when you hide I faint with fear.
Have mercy, Christ; Lord hear my prayer.

When I was sad you made me dance,
And when I mourned you made me wear
Gladness and joy, my freedom clothes.
Then help me, Christ; have mercy, Lord.

If I should die and go to hell
Yet even there I'd know your truth.
Lifelong your love; so evening tears
Soon disappear when morning comes.

Then sing to Christ, you friends of Christ,
Join me to praise the holy one.
My heart now sings – it never stops –
Praise to my Lord, Jesus my God.

7 PRAISE THE LORD (117)

This psalm is the shortest chapter in the Bible and is a little gem, containing much in few words. Matthew Henry says that it is short and sweet, but is to be sung for its sweetness rather than for its shortness. Jesus used it at the last supper.

All the heathen, all the nations, and we ourselves, are invited to praise God. Paul quotes these words in the letter to the Romans to show that the gospel is to be preached to all peoples, and that the Church is not for white persons only. But why do we have to be *told* to praise God?

B. K. Cunningham, unable to sleep one night, got up and looked out of the window. Human noises were hushed, the moon was full, the sky was bright with stars, the scent of flowers came up from the garden, the breeze had a breath of rain in it, a dog was barking in the distance, and he felt that God was close to him and that he was glad to be awake. And he remarked: 'I said as much of the Benedicite as I could remember and went back to bed.'

The Benedicite is the hymn which begins: 'Bless the Lord, all works of the Lord: sing praise to him and highly exalt him for ever.' It goes on to exhort all the natural world and all the human world to praise God. The works of nature honour God poetically by being what they are, tributes to the beauty and power of his creative energy. But they cannot praise God in words and feelings as we can. Agnostics have no God to praise, but praise should come easily to the believer. Perhaps the reason why we have to be reminded of it is, not only that we are so preoccupied with our own concerns that we forget about God, but also that, even if we praised God all day long, we should never be able to do this adequately because he is beyond all praise.

There is a poem in the book Ecclesiasticus which expresses this well:

> However much we say, we cannot exhaust our theme;
> to put it in a word: the Lord is all.
> Where can we find the skill to sing his praises?
> For he is greater than all his works.
> The Lord is terrible and very great,
> and marvellous is his power.
> Honour the Lord to the best of your ability,
> and he will still be high above all praise.
> Summon all your strength to declare his greatness,
> and be untiring, for the most you can do will fall short.
> Has anyone ever seen him, to be able to describe him?
> Can anyone praise him as he truly is?
> We have seen but a small part of his works,
> and there remain many mysteries greater still.
> (43.27-32 NEB)

Although we can never praise him perfectly we can try, and we can never say too often – provided that we mean it – Alleluia, praise the Lord. The psalmist gives two reasons why we should do so. First because of God's merciful kindness towards us. He has redeemed us, or we could put it more simply by saying 'because he loves us'. It is not that we as God's favourites are entitled to invite the world to praise him, but we are so grateful for his love that we want everyone we meet to share it with us, that they may praise him too. Love is the essence of his being and, great as our sins are, his love is greater. 'Where sin increased', Paul tells us, 'grace abounded all the more.' As another psalm says: 'Look how high the heaven is in comparison with the earth . . . so far hath he set our sins from us.' The Church is to be the nucleus of a new order which will draw together all the nations in penitence and praise.

The other reason for praising God is his truth – which means here his faithfulness, his trustworthiness. God is always consistent with his nature. His actions are never arbitrary, he does not blow hot and cold as we often do, and he is always true to himself.

We cannot depend in this way on human beings or on things, for life on earth is uncertain. A fine young man, moving into a position of effective Christian leadership, is taken from us through a small error of judgement on the highway. A building which has meant much to us has been torn down. A man whom I admired is steadily drinking himself into a state where he is no longer the man whom I used to know. A visitor, with whom I should have discussed a certain matter which stood between us, did not stay long, and I let the subject drift out to sea. But God does not change. The kingdom that he has given us is unshakeable, and what is unshaken will remain, so: Praise the Lord!

8 PRAISE (150)

The last psalm in the psalter is not about being sorry for sin, or asking for help in trouble, or thanksgiving or intercession. The last word goes to praise, and everything that breathes is urged again and again to praise the Lord, to sing alleluia. This psalm is an extended doxology for the whole psalter, the final chord of a great crescendo.

Where is God to be praised? In his sanctuary, which includes church buildings, though there are more sanctuaries than church buildings in the world, and many people find that they can be with the Lord and behold his beauty in nature or in their own homes. Yet the church building and what it stands for is important since, if churchgoing declines, personal religion generally declines with it.

Where is God to be praised? In his mighty firmament, which means in the vault of heaven where music rings through the spheres in cosmic praise – but it is also nearer home than that. God is to be praised in every place where his power reaches – in the post office, the forest, the rugby field, the cinema, the home, the beach, the place of work. All these are houses of the Lord, sanctuaries, holy places.

Why is God to be praised? Because of his mighty deeds in creating us, in loving us so much that he sent his Son to die for us and rise again, and in giving us his Holy Spirit to guide us and inspire us.

Why is God to be praised? Not only for what he has done for us, but for what he is in himself, for his exceeding greatness, for the beauty of his creative love.

How is God to be praised? With music and dancing. We can praise God with words, though words are inadequate to express our praise. Silence can help and so can music. The central part of this psalm sounds like a description of the Jerusalem Philharmonic Orchestra, impressive with its organ, strings, wind and percussion instruments, and human voices. The effect of it all is to lift us up to God that we may praise him, even though we do not fully understand what we are doing. One of the few intuitions on which almost everyone who writes about heaven is agreed is that there will be music there.

Dancing can also cause a lifting up of the heart. Some people think that Christians should not dance, in spite of all the dancing, including temple dancing, that there is in the Bible. Perhaps we pride ourselves on being sophisticated, on having got beyond dancing in church, but we could learn something about how to praise God from more primitive people who have not forgotten the spiritual meaning of the dance.

There are two ways of testing the quality of our praise. One is whether it clears the way for the mystery and the glory to come through. When Paul Tillich began work at the Union Theological Seminary in New York, his English was painfully inadequate. The President of the seminary, who attended Tillich's first course of lectures, commented: 'I don't understand what he says, but when I look at his face I believe.'

The other test is whether it transforms our daily lives. If it does, we shall have adapted our psalm to something that Paul wrote to the Galatians, by praising God with the fanfares of self-control, the lute of joy, the harp of peace, the timbrels of dancing love, the strings of gentleness, the pipes of patience, the cymbals of tuneful love, and the cymbals of triumphant love.

Who is to praise God? Everyone is to praise God, for praise is intended to be a universal activity. As the writer of the Book of Revelation says: 'I heard every creature in heaven and on earth and under the earth and in the sea, and all therein, saying: "To him who sits upon the throne and to the Lamb be blessing and honour and glory and might for ever and ever." '

Who is to praise God? 'Let everything that breathes praise the Lord.' This means every living creature that is capable of doing so. I may be short of breath, or hold my breath, or speak with bated breath, or not have been taught to breathe correctly. I may say that I am breathless or out of breath, or that you have taken my breath away. But when I cease to breathe I cease to live. And as long as I have breath I should be using all the breath I have to praise the Lord.

Prayers in Time of Stress

9 WHY DO THE HEATHEN? (2)

Why do the heathen so furiously rage together? To those who know Handel's *Messiah* these words are familiar from the great bass air which is built upon them. Perhaps you are humming the tune as you read this. Why do the heathen so furiously rage together, and why do the people imagine a vain thing? The great ones of the earth, says the psalmist, stand up against God, trying to break through the security cordon which surrounds him. Secret conspiracy and open rebellion against him are both on the rampage.

In today's world we still hear the furious rage, the loud and angry uproar, as humans attempt to take over the government of God's world. There are terrorist threats in Ireland, southern Africa, and the Middle East, hijackings, murders, communism, the petrol shutoff, assassinations of presidents and prime ministers. A friend asked me: Where will it all end? And I had to answer: What reason have you for supposing that it ever will end?

But we need not turn to international events for examples of furious rage and rebellion against God, for there is enough frenzied anger in our own hearts. This may or may not appear outwardly, but it rises up at the injustices that are done to us, at the criticism and gossip we have to bear with, at the intractable problems which come at us like enemies, and at the impossible people with whom we are expected to co-operate. Where will it all end? Where indeed?

The psalm answers this question in the form of a fast moving drama. As I read between the lines it seems to me that we have arrived, perhaps in a dream, at a theatre in heaven. We have come, not knowing what play we are to see, but expecting to have comfortable seats in the stalls. To our horror, however, we find ourselves on stage, taking part in a production which is totally out of hand. Nothing has been rehearsed and everyone is charging wildly about the stage doing his own thing. We realize that we are involved in a surrealist representation of what the world is like today – the heathen so furiously raging together, and the people imagining a vain thing.

Our first reaction is to say that we are in the wrong place. We are not terrorists, murderers, or even politicians, and it is not our fault that the world is in a mess. But we are a part of the world, and we can never opt out of it. We are involved in everything that goes on here, and we cannot talk of the wicked as 'they', a class of people quite distinct from 'us', the decent people. When we feel like that, we had better attempt some corporate penitence for our share in the sins of the world.

This is what Christ himself did. Instead of standing apart from the people he came to save, he identified himself with them. He submitted to John's baptism although he himself had no sins to be washed away. When he died on the cross he became sin for us. He accepted his share in the world's failure.

Once we have got our bearings in this dream theatre, we realize that the stalls are empty, but that God is upstairs in the balcony. He appears to be a wild, barbaric, boisterous, violent, almost savage God, the God whom another psalmist once compared with 'a giant refreshed with wine'. And there he is, looking down at the stage, first with amused contempt at our foolish and feeble efforts, and then laughing his head off at them. 'He that dwelleth in heaven shall laugh them to scorn: the Lord shall have them in derision.'

In our superior way we protest that God is not like that. Christ has shown us that he is our Father, loving, considerate, and gentle. Although this is true, the psalmist is trying to say that the supreme ruler of the universe is not remote, olympian, heartless, like the God of the Greek mosaics. He is passionately concerned with all that we do, and he is our judge. This is not the whole truth about him, but it is a part of the truth which we must not forget.

To return to the play, after a time God finds our behaviour no longer amusing. The limit of his patience has been reached and he is so angry that we expect him to turn his machine-guns on us and to wipe us all out, and we think that our last hour has come.

But instead of that, God surprisingly orders us all off the stage, and Act 2 of the drama begins. He sends his Son – he sends Jesus, though the psalmist could not know who it was – to take over in our place. The Son did this so effectively that we find him enthroned, both at Bethlehem and on the cross, serene and triumphant, a Byzantine Christ reigning from the tree. No doubt these verses about 'the Son of God' – which are widely quoted in the New Testament – greatly influenced the way in which Christians came to think about Jesus and the power of his kingdom. Here again they are true as far as they go, but we have to remember that, in addition to being ruler of the world, Jesus is also the light of the world and the servant of the world.

It was an extraordinary way of re-establishing control. It is like a business which was on the rocks and, although everyone concerned with it was convinced that it was viable, they all, management consultants included, were unable to say what should be done. Then someone had the bright idea of calling in the chairman's son. He was a young man doing his army training but they got special leave for him. Certainly he was brilliant, but what could he hope to do when all the experts had failed? So it was when God's Son appeared. He was only a carpenter, Joseph's son, a man of sorrows and acquainted with grief. What could he hope to do? Christ's coming looked a curiously ineffective way of putting the world to rights, and yet God was never seen to be more wonderful than when he sent his Son to save us.

Jesus was recognized on earth by those who had eyes

to see him as the Son, the only Son of the Father, the master of the nations and the lord, not only of the Church, but of the world. During the temptations the devil took him up a mountain and showed him the kingdoms of the world in their glory and promised to give them to him if he would do homage for them. But those kingdoms belonged to Christ anyway, and he had no need to receive them at the devil's hand.

This psalm represents those who disobey Christ as being broken in pieces like a potter's vessel. In my first parish in south London we had a sideshow at our fêtes called 'Smashing up the happy home'. We begged parishioners to give us pieces of china that were cracked or broken or not needed any more, we set these things up on shelves, and we invited people to have a go at them for so much a wooden ball. It brought out the worst instincts of destruction and it brought in much money. I did not then realize that this was an ancient ceremony. At the coronation of the Israelite kings a row of earthenware jars was set up, and one was labelled Syria and one Russia and another China or whatever the chief enemies of the time happened to be. The king's bodyguard then threw things at these vessels until they were destroyed. This was saying in picture language that God would destroy the enemies of the new king.

We see Jesus, then, enthroned on the cross, enthroned in the glory of the resurrection, enthroned at the altar, enthroned in the hearts of men. Nothing can withstand the power of his love.

But this is not the end of the drama. Lest we think that we can sit back and say that, as Christ has overcome sin and death, there is nothing for us to do, the psalm goes on to issue warnings. We can see this third act of the play as being the act of the Holy Spirit, as the first act was about the Father and the second about the Son. The Holy Spirit now brings us on to the stage again. He speaks to us, teaches us, shows us what to do, and he is immensely patient with our clumsiness and our slowness.

He invites all rebels to submit and promises them freedom if they do so. We must not interpret this in triumphalist terms. We can be loyal to our Church, to its structure and its interests, in a worldly and selfish way. There is a sense in which God wants his Church, in the war against evil, to be militant and colonialist and nationalist, but we dare not use these words unless we have already understood that the Church is transcendent and supernatural, and that it exists only by the grace of God.

So we must worship and serve the Lord, and kiss his feet with all the reverence that we can show to him. This is true wisdom and the only learning that matters, especially for those who hold positions of responsibility.

This is the way to happiness and to the lovely beatitude with which the psalm ends: 'Blessed are all they that put their trust in him'. Any other way leads us back to the evil that is waiting for us in the dark corners, to the heathen so furiously raging together and to the people imagining a vain thing. Where will it all end? It ends at the empty tomb and the risen Lord and our participation in the life of the resurrection. On Good Friday Jesus said: 'It is finished.' On Easter Day he led those who had faith in him to share in the victory of the cross.

10 SHEPHERD AND HOST (23)

This is an immortal psalm and a great favourite among all Christians. As I read it, it comes out of a situation of anxiety, worry, and trouble. The writer lived on the edge of the Arabian desert where life was hard, and where it is still hard as we know from pictures of the fighting there in recent years. Would he find food and shelter? Would he get lost? Would he be able to overcome his fears, especially when he had to go through the valley of the shadow of death, that dangerous ravine where wild animals were known to live?

We have all been through situations of anxiety, and some people seem to live permanently in an anxious state. They worry about themselves, about their health, about the success of their work, about their relationship with their neighbour. Or they are anxious for others. What can be done about this loved one who is desperately ill and yet the doctors cannot diagnose what is wrong? Will this young man be able to hold down a job? Will this girl ever get through the examination for which she has worked so hard and twice failed? How can this man save his marriage from going on the rocks? What can be done about that child who is out of control? When life seems empty and meaningless, is suicide a reasonable way out? Is it safe to walk about the streets after dark? Is it safe to die? This psalm can be applied to all our anxieties, and its meaning grows with experience.

In that situation of anxiety something happened to the psalmist. He saw God – in fact he saw Jesus, though he did not know who he was – as the good shepherd. We are told that the idea of the good shepherd is out of date. When city dwellers in South African cities go into the country, the only shepherds whom they see are small herdboys, and it is hard to derive much spiritual enlightenment from them. But even if the image itself is out of date, the ideas for which it stands are completely contemporary.

The good shepherd is someone who has the answer to our anxieties and who puts new life into us when we seem to be dead. He gives us a fresh start when we are stuck. He loves us. He protects us with skill and devotion. He sees that we are short of nothing. He is authoritative, but we gladly accept his authority because we know that it works in our best interests.

One special aspect of the shepherd's work is his guidance. 'He brings me forth in the paths of righteousness' – he guides us along the road to eternal life. He does this 'for his name's sake' – because that is the sort of God he is. Similarly a man may speak with gratitude of 'my doctor', who has guided him back to life through a dangerous illness. Often the good shepherd guides us through other people – a teacher, a confessor, a counsellor, a psychiatrist, a friend, even a policeman – but it is the good shepherd himself who does the guiding.

The psalmist does not tell us what form this experience took, and that is fortunate, for God visits us in different ways, and there is no one pattern which must always be followed. He comes through the sacraments, the Bible, prayer, poetry, music, nature, a pentecostal experience, conversion, or simply through the happenings of daily life. What matters is not the way in which he comes but the fact that he comes.

If we know that the good shepherd is with us, loving, protecting, guiding, working within us, we shall be confident that everything is all right even though our anxieties and problems continue or actually increase. God may bring us into green pastures or he may bring us into the valley of the shadow. Jesus has not abolished death but all is well because he is with us in death. He may lead us to the waters of comfort – perhaps the psalmist is thinking of the quiet waters of a dam constructed in a rocky wadi – or he may lead us into a raging torrent. A social worker among dropouts or a full-time hospital chaplain is not expected to know much about green pastures and calm waters, but if such lives are hid with Christ in God they are full of quiet confidence.

One of my favourite quotations – its source is unknown to me – is that, although we do not know what the future holds (and we are glad that we do not know this), we do know who holds the future. It is because Christ died on the cross to save us and because he rose again that we are given triumphant faith. We face the future, whatever it may hold, with courage, because we face it with Christ.

There is a further thought in this psalm, for in the last two verses – which form a little psalm within the great psalm – the picture changes. We stop thinking of God as the good shepherd, and we see him as the generous host, and ourselves as guests in his home.

Here again we start with a situation of anxiety and danger, for there are enemies, 'those who trouble us'. Some maintain that, the more Christian our lives are, the more enemies we shall have. This is doubtful because, although positive Christian witness is offensive to the world, the beauty of Christian love always wins over some enemies.

The psalmist was being attacked, and he thought that he was done for, when he saw God – in fact he saw Jesus, though he did not know who he was – as one who offered an unexpected refuge in his own house. The enemies could not pursue him there, for he was now in a place of diplomatic immunity, in an embassy perhaps, though embassies are not the safe places that once they were. He felt secure there even though his enemies were glaring at him through the garden fence. Here he received lavish hospitality both in food and in lodging. The oil which anointed his head was not the holy oil of consecration, but the perfumed oil which was used at grand banquets. For us this has eucharistic overtones since, when we are in the Lord's house and at the Lord's table, our cup – the chalice of salvation – is full, and we are extravagantly entertained.

Our response again is confidence, even though we still have to face those who trouble us, for we know that God's lovingkindness and mercy will follow us all the days of our life and that we shall dwell in the house of the Lord and be with the Lord for ever – here in the life of the Church and afterwards in paradise.

But however much attention we pay to these last two verses, it is for the image of the good shepherd that we mainly treasure this psalm. It is not easy to be a good shepherd as anyone knows who has tried to exercise pastoral care of any sort. In church the bishop carries a pastoral staff to show that he is the chief shepherd in his diocese, but the fact that we can speak of a good shepherd warns us that there can be bad shepherds also. There is only one good shepherd, and what it cost Jesus to be that we shall never know. His love drove him to look more like a lost sheep than a shepherd at Calvary, though he never was a lost sheep, but always the lamb of God. This double idea of Jesus as both the good shepherd and the lamb of the sacrifice is dramatically brought out by John the theologian when he says: 'The Lamb in the midst of the throne will be their shepherd, and he will guide them to springs of living water.'

11 FAITH IN SUFFERING (88)

This is a psalm of unrelieved suffering and gloom which raises many questions that can be answered only at Calvary. For the Christian, God who is hidden in suffering is also revealed in suffering, and so we face suffering with wonder and awe, knowing that it brings us into God's presence and that, even if our suffering gets worse, God will never let us go.

But the psalmist was not aware of what Jesus was to do with suffering, and he may even have died before his own suffering ended, and perhaps he knew no joy at any time in his life, nor saw any possible way of escape. So this sad singer of Israel tells of God's terrible silence, and sees only darkness, darkness, before him all his days. The last word in the psalm should correctly be 'darkness'. Life for him was a long death, and yet he was no pessimistic grumbler for in the darkness he went on crying to God, the mysterious, the inaccessible, the incomprehensible. He desired above all to have communion with God and, although apparently he could not have it, it was always God to whom he spoke throughout his ordeal. God had forsaken him, but he was still *his* God.

This psalm is like an autumn day; there is mist and rain, and the movement is towards winter, and yet there is a glory in it, for faith comes through the near despair. There is also some incoherence, and this is not surprising for, when we are going through an ordeal, we do not normally stop to analyse it neatly into its component parts or to document the situation with the aid of a computer. We call out spontaneously for help according to the state of our feelings; and these may vary from hour to hour.

As we read this psalm, it is easy for us to apply it to the sufferings of the Lord, and to recognize his voice as he calls to his Father from Calvary, where the narrow walls of his passion hem him in like a prison – 'I am so fast in prison that I cannot get forth.' The God who is addressed throughout is the 'Lord of my salvation', my personal saviour; and the prayer is for admission into his presence. No soul was ever so full of trouble as Christ's was when he called on his Father by night in Gethsemane and by day at Calvary. His life seemed near to hell, and he was counted as dead and useless. 'My soul is exceedingly sorrowful', he said, and he warned his followers that they would be hated by everyone because of him.

He was 'free among the dead' – a very striking phrase, the original reference probably being to someone who was adrift and homeless among the dead. If we accept the tradition that Job was a leper, we see in him the picture of a man who was literally free among dead men, who had freehold rights only in a cemetery. For Christ it means that he freely chose to die, since his death was not something that was imposed upon him against his will. His freedom also means that he was not bound by death and corruption.

But even at Calvary, and even when he lay in the grave, Jesus was always the Beloved Son, never out of remembrance of his Father's love. In the lowest pit, in the darkness, in the deep, there was for him no indignation or vexation. As we read these words, we hear breakers on a rocky coast, and it seems as if we are drowning in a lonely sea. Troubles tend to feel like this anyway, but if we who live on this side of the cross can believe in Christ's saving power, we shall, like Christopher in the legend, come through the tempest to find that the burden under which we were staggering is the Christchild himself.

To be separated from friends, and indeed to be hated by them, was another experience that came to Christ and that comes to his followers also – to a student in a segregated society who openly witnesses to justice, to a nun who enters a community against the wishes of her family, to a priest who preaches the gospel in a communist country. The words 'my sight faileth' remind us of Christ's blindfolding, and perhaps also of his tears.

In verses 10-12 there are questions about death and resurrection which all seem to expect a negative reply and to be appropriate to the mood of Holy Saturday, but which are gloriously answered by the events of Easter Day with its wonders and praise and love and righteousness, the remembrance of which will never fade.

And so the psalmist is still praying, and he will go on praying, although it seemed as if God had hidden his face from him. ('My God, my God, why hast thou forsaken me?') God often delays answering prayers, or he answers them in a way which surprises us, but he always hears our requests. He never abhors our soul and, when it feels as if he is doing just that, this is another warning about the difference between feeling and fact.

The misery and the trouble that had been going on 'from my youth up' remind us that Christ's passion did not start in Holy Week. It was lifelong, for its starting point was in the manger, but its climax came at the end when, with hardly any friends or lovers, he trod the winepress alone. Here is an experience which we cannot share for, even in our deepest distress, even in death, we are never alone since the Lord is with us always. But suffering is also with us always, and what that means for us now depends on how deeply suffering is biting into us at this moment. (Even if we have practically nothing to suffer ourselves, we can always enter into someone else's suffering.)

Suffering is a mystery beyond our powers of explanation. If we have to pass an examination on its theory we shall fail, but God may enable us to be more successful in the practical, because what matters most is our response to suffering. We are not to rebel against it, or scream at

God for allowing a teenage suicide, or a tumour on the brain, or a little child to be run over when crossing the road. We are not to pretend that we can control suffering or claim, with Henley, that we are the master of our fate and the captain of our soul. We are not to be resigned about it either, saying that it is fate, Kismet, and that you cannot get out of the way of a bomb which has your name written on it; or that it is a judgement upon us.

We are rather to accept it patiently and if possible gladly, because this is the way of the cross. As I recite this psalm I become confused in my mind about two things – what it meant to Christ and what it means to me. Even to compare my sufferings with his seems conceited and yet Paul tells us that Christ allows us to share in his passion through our sufferings. Then I think that perhaps I should try to forget my sufferings and contemplate Jesus only – and yet how can I do that when this psalm expresses clearly what I sometimes feel?

What we are sure about is that Jesus loves us so much that he deliberately chose suffering as the means of redeeming the world; and that he calls us now to take up the cross and to imitate him, especially as he 'stretches forth his hands' in acts of compassion and in prayer.

Jesus crucified and risen is with us always but, because there are times when it seems almost impossible to believe that, this psalm is important as encouraging us to go on praying through the darkness, and as assuring us that to pray without receiving any apparent response from God is itself a sign of faith.

12 CHAOS OVERCOME (93)

This psalm proclaims in a powerful, dramatic way that 'the Lord is king'. Perhaps it was composed after the return from Babylon when, with Jerusalem in ruins, it looked to the Israelites as if God had thrown away all signs of royalty and had abdicated.

The psalm speaks of floods that rise, that lift up their voice, that lift up their waves, that rage horribly. These floods stand for our oppressors. The Jews of the Bible with a few exceptions hated and feared the sea, and it is not surprising that they made it a symbol of the hostile powers. Now all this is changed, and modern Israelis crowd on the beaches west of Tel-Aviv, and the liner Queen Elizabeth II could sail into Ashdod harbour on the sabbath day without causing more than nominal murmurings.

If the immediate thought of the psalm is the triumphant restoration of the kingdom after the exile, there is also in it the deeper thought of God as the king of creation. The Jews were fascinated by the myths which they found in Babylon about Tiamat the dragon goddess of chaos, and the god Marduk who defeated her, and there are references to this in the Old Testament. So they came to believe that the world was originally in a state of chaos with no security or stability anywhere. In fact an 'out of order' notice could have been hung over the whole universe. Then God fought against the chaotic powers, defeated them, and showed his royal power by creating the world as we now know it.

We do not have to believe the Babylonian legend, but we must praise God for the wonderful way in which he created the world and in which he sustains it. We can enter into the spirit of this psalm as it speaks to us out of a situation where chaos and failure have been overcome because God entered that situation; and now there is new life and great joy. God has re-established order and made the round world so *sure*. Instead of scrapping mankind for their sin, as nearly happened at the time of the flood, God saved us and made us sure. Paul had the vision of this ultimately happening in its complete perfection when he saw creation delivered from corruption and brought into the glorious liberty of the children of God. This, as Peter said, is the Easter message, that by God's great mercy we have been born anew to a living hope by the resurrection of Jesus Christ from the dead. The new creation is a victory for the powers of order.

Chaos was experienced during the Captivity too, when it seemed that the moral order of the universe had been shaken. The floods were risen, the prince of this world had taken charge, and, as Jesus said in Gethsemane: 'This is your hour and the power of darkness.' It was the day of what Paul called 'the principalities, the powers, the rulers of the darkness of this world, the spiritual wickedness in high places.' This chaos was also reduced to order when God brought his exiled people home.

When the psalm says 'The Lord is King', this means for Christians that Christ reigns from the tree. There he is clothed with flesh, clothed with our human nature, clothed with the power of weakness, and yet at the same time he is eternal in his divine majesty. The king has 'put on glorious apparel', and everyone can see that he really is the king. When the psalm describes him as the best dressed king and as the leader in the fashion stakes, it is only saying in picture language that nothing is too good for God. The seat that has been prepared for the Lord is at his Father's right hand, and there he is glorified with the glory that he had before the world was. For, as Paul says, God 'has highly exalted him and bestowed on him the name which is above every name, that at the name of Jesus every knee should bow'.

Perhaps we shall understand this psalm better if we think

of some contemporary situations. Some years ago I came up the English channel in a cargo ship in a force ten gale, with mighty waves breaking almost to the level of the bridge, the wind howling terribly, the clouds down to sea level, spray like driving snow, great mountains and valleys appearing in the sea. I happen to be a good sailor, and I found all this exhilarating, but that was largely because I did not realize how chaotic the situation was. There was a real possibility that the ship – built in wartime – might have broken up, and it was a gale in which no lifeboat could have been launched. I understood this only when the storm began to abate, and the captain came down from the bridge, his face an ashen grey colour, and he looking ten years older. This helped me to see a little better how much it cost Christ to bring us through the chaos at Calvary.

We see evidence of chaos today in the pollution, the exploitation, violence, and injustice which afflict in some degree every country. But God still sits on his throne and he still judges the world from that throne and he is – may he give us eyes to see this – all the time bringing order out of our man-made chaos, and wanting to use us as his instruments in bringing this about.

The same is true of our personal lives, for we all know what it means to live through a situation of chaos. A man was taking his family for a jaunt in the car on Saturday afternoon. They were a happy quartette, without a care in the world, when suddenly a lorry swerved into them, killing the wife, disabling the husband and doing no one knew what mental injury to the children. A man who was generous with his wealth and his time in the service of others was highly honoured in his community until it was discovered that for years he had been defrauding his firm. Overnight he became bankrupt and a nobody, with his life a chaotic ruin. A religious who had been moderately fulfilled in her community for years suddenly found that the whole thing was meaningless. In *The Gulag Archipelago* Alexander Solzhenitsyn tells of Russians living normal lives who were arrested by the secret police and who realized that they would not emerge for at least ten years.

These are dramatic examples, but similar things happen to us, even if it is only the collapse of a plan we have made, or the muddles we get into, or the apparent hopelessness of ever realizing the ideals that have been set before us.

When we are in such a situation, what we have to do is to cling on in faith to the conviction that God still sits on his throne, and that he can and will bring order out of our home-made chaos. Then we must take our chaos to him, and spread it out helplessly before him – not trying to cover it up or disguise it, and not pretending that we ourselves could deal with it if only we took the time and trouble to do so – and ask him to use his divine power to bring his divine order into the situation. All Christian experience down the ages unites to assure us that, if we do this, we shall find that the Lord is mightier than the floods which threaten us, that his testimonies are very sure, and that he is our king for ever.

13 IN EXILE (137)

In the first six verses of this moving psalm, we hear the mournful cry of the exile, the dispossessed, and the homeless, yearning for their own country as they prayed by the river Euphrates, or perhaps by one of the canals near Babylon. In their deep sorrow they remembered Jerusalem with affection all day long, and they would have preferred to be struck dumb rather than be given the power to forget her. But they could not sing there the Lord's songs, as their arrogant captors mockingly demanded, because to sing the songs of Sion would not have been the right way to entertain the destroyers of Sion. It would have been like Belshazzar using consecrated vessels at his dinner party; it would have been throwing pearls before swine. So they were unable to enjoy themselves in Babylon; and their harps, no longer of any use to them, were hung up on the poplar trees.

Whether it is the Jew longing for Jerusalem, or the migratory labourer sighing for home, or the displaced person in a strange land, or the Christian in an evil world longing for his true country in heaven, it is loyalty to their faith which keeps them going even in the day of humiliation.

The only criticism that we can raise against the Jewish exiles – and should we do as well as they did in similar circumstances? – is that they ought to have praised God out of season as well as in it. This is especially true of us who are Christians for, exiles and homeless though we are, we can hardly help singing one of the songs of Sion when we know that Christ is sharing our exile and our homelessness with us.

But what about the second half of the psalm? Here is intense hatred of the Edomites, the brothers who had helped their enemies, and blind rage against the Babylonians. There is no question here of loving and forgiving enemies, but only a horror picture of bitter denunciation in depths of passion. They are actually praying God to remember their enemies for evil, to take revenge upon them, to repay them in their own coin, and to bless anyone who killed their children.

It shocks us to hear this praise of murder and of the principle of two eyes for an eye, to see the sublime and the vicious side by side, a beauty queen and a tramp sitting on the same desegregated bench in the park. The discord is unbearable, and we want to censor these last verses and throw them out of the Bible.

C. S. Lewis has his own way of justifying this savage prayer, but I find him more ingenious than convincing:[1]

> I know things in the inner world which are like babies; the infantile beginnings of small indulgencies, small resentments which may one day become dipsomania or settled hatred, but which woo us and wheedle us with special pleadings, and seem so tiny, so helpless, that in resisting them we feel we are being cruel to animals. They begin whimpering to us 'I don't ask much, but', or 'I had at least hoped', or 'You owe yourself *some* consideration'. Against all such pretty infants (the dears have such winning ways) the advice of the Psalm is the best. Knock the little bastards' brains out. And 'blessed' he who can, for it's easier said than done.

I can find no way to defend the use of these verses in church, though in my private devotions I know that, when I condemn them, I am also passing judgement on the contemptible rages which rise up in my heart, and I am meeting a challenge to see myself honestly and not as my fantasies suggest that I am. This is what I am like – a

[1] *Reflections on the Psalms* (Fontana), pp.113-14.

mixture of good and evil – and this is what society is like, and what the Church itself is like.

But in this mixup evil never has the last word. Into whatever depths of sin we have sunk, Christ lifts us up again, and he assures us that in the end good will prevail. This is presumably what our office books intend when they add a Gloria to every psalm, so that this one ends, not with 'stones', but with the praise of God.

14 TRUSTING IN GOD (91)

Before we look at this wonderful expression of personal trust in a personal God, there are some misunderstandings to be cleared up.

First we must realize who is speaking. Most of the psalm is spoken to us in God's name by a priest who assures us that God is looking after us and that we are not to be afraid. Then there are two choruses in which we respond by saying to God: You are my hope. But in the last three verses God addresses us, not through a priest, but directly; here the 'he' and 'him' means 'you' and 'me'.

Then there is in the psalm an attitude to enemies which is unchristian. The gloating over the punishment of the ungodly and the smug confidence that we are not as other men would be better omitted in view of the divine command to love our enemies.

There is also a false view of suffering. The psalm suggests that the believer will either not fall into danger or become sick, or else will recover or escape rapidly. No evil will ever happen to us! Even if the pestilence kills off ten thousand people all round us, it will not touch us. But in fact God's servants do fall sick, the plague is not afraid of entering a Christian house, and the foot of the faithful is often hurt by the stones; these things should not take us by surprise. A woman who suffered from severe migraine was anointed by a priest but, because he did not explain the position to her, she thought that this guaranteed her cure and when another migraine occurred she lost her faith. What God offers to those who trust him is the power to accept and endure suffering, and the power to prevent it from harming our inmost soul; and it is only in that sense that we can understand the promises that are made here.

The experience lying behind this psalm is that of weakness and defencelessness in the face of trouble, and most people can identify something of that in their own experience. The images are mainly oriental and need to be translated. The snare of the hunter could mean death on the road, the noisome pestilence a cancer ward, the terror by night air raids, the arrow by day a city mugger, the plague a killer influenza, the lion and the adder hostile and aggressive people we have to live with – or spiritual problems such as the inability to pray, failure in work, or perplexity before the new ideas which bombard us in the Church.

In such situations the message of this psalm is that God is present and that he is our hope. Paul found that God worked through him *especially* in times of weakness, for Jesus had said to him: 'My grace is sufficient for you, for my power is made perfect in weakness', and when he was weak then he was strong. God says to us: 'I am with you in trouble.' He does not promise to get us out of trouble, but he does promise to come into the trouble with us, as a good friend, and that makes the trouble bearable. God said to Julian of Norwich: You may be afflicted, but you will not be overcome.

This assumes that when we are in trouble we turn to God, as the prodigal son did, and then God meets us halfway, delivers us, sets us up, provides us with shade from the heat, becomes our stronghold, house of defence, shield, buckler, and protecting wings (this last piece of symbolism appealed to the Lord also). He sends guardian angels who carry us like a child in their arms and who express what Weiser calls God's 'motherly solicitude'. These images are also oriental and need translation. Perhaps we should say that God gives us protection like a burglar alarm, security like a bank, comfort like an airconditioner, transport like a chauffeur-driven limousine. We shall not forget, however, that we still live in a world of burglars, hold-ups, extremes of heat and cold, and accidents. It is God and God alone who will see us through all our troubles, and I dare to call him '*my* God'.

It is implied, especially in the opening verses, that it is in the hours of worship and prayer that we receive the strength to overcome. The trusting man has serenity of mind because he is at home with God, lives a life of inward communion with God, and always comes back from his business in the world to God. Once we realize that God is with us in our trouble, love overcomes our fears, and we share in the exuberant trust of this psalmist.

The opposite of fear is not courage but faith, and it is faith that gives us courage and makes us strong. Yet trust is a gift from God which has to be used under certain conditions and within defined boundaries. It is not the same as sitting down and letting God do everything for us, since faith must be responsible. 'The young lion and the dragon shalt thou tread under thy feet' – it is you who have to do the treading. Satan quoted two of these verses at the Temptation: 'He shall give his angels charge over thee, to keep thee in all thy ways. They shall bear thee in their hands, that thou hurt not thy foot against a stone.' But Jesus – because he was a responsible person – refused to jump off the temple roof.

We should not ask God to look after us if we refuse to do what we can to look after ourselves, nor ask him to do for us what we can do for ourselves. There is a story of two missionary ladies on safari through the East African bush at the turn of the century. They had become separated from their porters when they heard the noise of elephants close by. Without delay, in spite of her long skirts, one climbed a tall tree, but the other dropped to her knees in prayer at the foot of the tree. Which one acted as the more responsible Christian?

The last three verses of the psalm are the great ones, for here God speaks to us and gives us his blessing:

I rescue all who cling to me,
I protect whoever knows my name,

I answer everyone who invokes me,
I am with them when they are in trouble;
I bring them safety and honour,
I give them life, long and full,
And I show them how I can save.[1]

As Paul says, God allows us to be tempted, or tested, but never above our powers for, when the test comes, he will provide a way out by enabling us to sustain it. Consequently nothing can separate from the love of Christ those who know his name and who love him and who pray to him.

For our own devotion we can turn these verses round and, paraphrasing them a little, make them our prayer to God:

Lord, I love you.
I know you, though not as you know me.
You always answer me when I call you.
You always look after me.
You are always with me in trouble.
You have honoured me by making me your child.
You have given me eternal life.
You have shown me how you can save.

[1] Jerusalem Bible translation.

15 GOD IS WITH US (46)

Twice, and originally three times, this psalm has as its chorus:

The Lord of hosts is with us,
The God of Jacob is our refuge.

Martin Luther based a famous hymn on these words:

A safe stronghold our God is still,
A trusty shield and weapon.

As Christians we may prefer to say:

The almighty God is with us,
The Father of Jesus Christ is our refuge.

Or we could condense it all into the single word of the Christmas message: Emmanuel – God is with us.

These words bring great confidence. Whenever Luther heard any depressing news, he used to say: Let us sing Psalm 46! It is a psalm of trust in God alone as our saviour. It includes confidence about the future, since God says: 'I *will* be exalted among the heathen, and I will be exalted in the earth.' But there is also present confidence, in the face of natural forces which we cannot control – earthquakes, storms, and drought – and in the face of human forces which we fail to control – the heathen making much ado and the kingdoms suffering upheaval. We can be confident because –

The Lord of hosts is with us,
The God of Jacob is our refuge.

God is with us always. He is with us in our praying for, as this psalm says, he is in the midst of his Church, in the holy place of his tabernacle. This may seem a glimpse of the obvious, as we tend to assume that this is the one time when we are sure that God is with us, especially when we are present at the Eucharist. But this psalm also says: Be still and know that I am God. Unless we are still and listen to God, we may be in his presence and yet forget all about him. Presumably at Pentecost there were many people in Jerusalem who went about their ordinary affairs without having any idea that the Holy Spirit had arrived. In Gethsemane the chosen disciples simply went to sleep in the very presence of Christ. How they must have kicked themselves afterwards for having missed their share in that immortal experience! And all because they were unable to be still and know that he was God. Similarly we can come to church and receive communion and still be unaware that we are in the presence of God. 'It is high time', says Paul, 'to awake out of sleep . . . for the night is far spent and the day is at hand.' So that we must wake up and know that God is with us.

This of course is the Advent message, and I was preaching one December on these lines, when I noticed that the choir, who were seated immediately in front of me, were trying to suppress their giggles. I wondered what I had said, until I glanced round and saw the Rector deeply and seraphically asleep in his stall. That was an extreme case, but it is always easy to take a spiritual siesta in church, to indulge in daydreams, to give your real attention to a problem that is worrying you, instead of worshipping God.

But God is also with us in our working. It is our privilege to go with God, whom we encounter in our praying, out into our everyday world. As the psalmist says, God is concerned with the wars and misunderstandings between nations and groups and, we can add, between races and classes. God makes these factions to cease, by educating us for peaceful change and, if we cannot accept his teaching, it may be for violent change as well. He certainly wants his love to flow out through us, wherever it is that we are working, in reconciliation.

The apostles discovered at Pentecost this truth that God

is with us in our work. For them God was not a distant God; he was in the room where they were sitting, and in the street where people came running together. And because he is with us in our work, we must work with him and in such a way as to please him.

An underground manager of a goldmine was one day doing a routine inspection when he received a report that work was at a standstill in a certain area. On arriving there he found a large group of black miners sitting on the ground, and a white miner standing before them with a Bible in his hand. He was reading it and expounding it and leading them in prayer. The manager lost his temper, shouted, ordered them back to work, and even lashed out at one man who gave him a cheeky answer. Subsequently he was filled with remorse that he, a communicant, should have broken up a prayer meeting in anger. It seemed to me that he was wrong to shout at them, for violence is never the best way to settle a dispute. (That after all is why we object to terrorism.) But on the main point he was surely right. Those men were being paid to do a job of work and, if they were Christians, they should have been earning their pay, and God would then have been with them in their work. It was splendid that they should pray together, but they could have done that before or after work.

God is also with us in our loving. We know all too well that the cost of living is continually escalating, and obviously there are two ways of facing this situation. If our income is fixed and we have no means of increasing it, we must cut down on our expenses – make that dress last a little longer, do with simpler holidays, or reduce our luxuries. (This does not, however, help those who are living below the breadline anyway.) The other way is to increase our income – by working longer hours, sending a spouse out to work, or more probably receiving an increase in salary from a sympathetic employer.

The same is true of the cost of loving. There is little doubt that this is also going up every day. Forgiveness and compassion become much more expensive in the context of the cruelty, suffering, injustice, and violence that are on the increase all around us. One way to face this situation is to cut down on our loving – to say that we will not even attempt to love all our neighbours, but only our own family and two or three especially close friends. That would be terrible because, if we persisted in it, we should become steadily less human. The other way is to go to the Lord and ask him for a wage increase, for more of that love which we so badly need, and he will give us as much of it as we are capable of receiving and passing on.

This thought was in the mind of our psalmist when he pictured the presence of God as a river which poured out of the temple, quietly flowing, bringing new life to the desert, and making everyone happy. The grace of God is thus like the streams that came out of paradise; and Ezekiel was later to take up the same idea.

But if God's love is to flow, like a river of grace, through us to other people, this will have some definite consequences. For example, we shall love our neighbours so much that we shall be ready to make sacrifices for Christian unity; we shall give more generously to others of our money and time; we shall be willing to serve, not only the nice people whom we like enormously, but also the needy whom we do not find attractive. For the Lord of hosts is with us in our praying and in our working and in our loving. The God of Jacob is our refuge – always.

16 JUDGEMENT (50)

This wonderful psalm, so close to the spirit of Christ, is the kind of writing that we should expect from one of the great prophets, and that is high praise. It is a vision of judgement which is also a vision of salvation.

The setting is a lawcourt and the scene opens with the arrival of the judge who for us is Jesus, since the Father 'has given him authority to execute judgement because he is the Son of man'. It is not surprising that this is an Advent psalm, and we can interpret it of either the first or the second coming of the Lord.

Here as at Sinai the judge comes in lightning and storm and consuming fire. In this encounter with the living God the fire will turn out to be that of pentecostal love, but this is not obvious at the start to the defendants – and the defendants are, we find to our surprise, ourselves. We judge the government, the world in general, and our neighbours in particular, but now it is we who stand in the dock before the judge, and we are terrified by his august presence.

In these prosaic days we find 'theophanies' – the appearances of God in the thunder and the glory – difficult to understand, but we are foolish if we suppose that God's judgements are no longer to be taken seriously. He is still mighty and terrible and to be feared, but now in different ways. His coming in judgement in a political crisis, in an economic crash, or in a confrontation with our own conscience, is, if we realize what is happening, equally alarming.

Here is a God who is often silent, rarely screaming at us to stop doing whatever we are doing, and sometimes not answering us when we want him to speak. His silence is deceptive, however, if it tempts us to believe that we are getting away with things. But now in judgement God breaks what Weiser calls his uncanny silence, and his voice carries to the end of the world.

There was no question of our being picked up before the trial by unsympathetic police or being locked up in a distant prison. The cosmic Christ meets us where we are, on our own ground, in the church to which we are proud to belong and which we consider to be so beautiful. For in spite of everything we are the Lord's own people – he calls us his saints! – and we have made a covenant with him.

In a passage full of poetic symbolism, heaven and earth, which were there before man was created and which have watched us develop our amazing expertise at sinning, are called to give evidence against us. The heavens praise God as a just and impartial judge, not because they are hoping to get something out of him or because they are being accused – for they have always accomplished perfectly the functions for which they were created – but because they know how things really stand with us.

The judge is also the prosecutor, a doubling up of functions which could not achieve impartiality in a human court, but God is truth. He says: 'I am God, even thy God', and we can only reply: Yes, you are God, even my God – now in the battle of life here on earth and eventually, we hope and pray, in the peace of the beatific vision.

The first charge is that we have failed in our worship which has been formal and unreal. How could it come about that, although we have gone through the correct motions of church attendance and regular prayers, we have not given God the devotion of our hearts? Why within the context of the cult is there so little personal religion, so little understanding of the inner nature of our faith? Sometimes our motivation has been wrong, for we have tried to bribe God with gifts, or to patronize him by taking occasional notice of him. This is a sign of our failure to realize that he is the owner of everything, including church buildings and their furnishings. He does not depend on us or on our prayerbook, hymnbook, or Bible. In these days we are unlikely to imagine that God has a serious longing for veal, lamb, or chicken – for the cordon bleu and the cognac – but sometimes we forget that he has no need of us at all. Certainly he is not impressed by the smells, whether of incense in church or of coffee in the hall afterwards. According to Tertullian, the Lord said: 'The eternal God shall neither hunger nor thirst.'

One morning I was in a convent chapel. Dawn was still half an hour away, and the only light came from an oil lamp before the sacrament and from the paraffin lamps, turned down low, which made it just possible to find the way about. The place was apparently empty but, at the ringing of the bell for the office and the turning up of the lamps, black-robed figures arose, as if from the dead, in several places. It seemed to me that here was true worship, unadvertised, dedicated, a God-centred silence which led into God-centred praise.

What God looks for is the sacrifice and burnt offering of ourselves, body, soul, and spirit, and for the Christian 'the sacrifice of thanksgiving' has a eucharistic flavour. It is not saying a thankyou though it may cost something to say that, nor doing a thankyou though it may cost more to do that; for in the eucharistic sacrifice we plead before the Father the merits of his Son's sufferings and we offer ourselves in him.

The second charge is that we have failed in obedience to God, that in spite of religious appearances our lives are hypocritical. In church we have said prayers, sung hymns, and given alms, and then we have got on with our favourite sins. Two of the instances given by the psalmist – stealing and adultery – may not seem to concern us personally, though stealing includes marginal dishonesty, and adultery impure thoughts. We may think it an exaggeration to say, even in this permissive age, that these sins are common among church people. But it is doubtful whether any of us is innocent of what seems to be the most serious sin of all – it is referred to four times – spoken words of wickedness, deceit, criticism, and slander. It is easy to be a preacher who does not listen to his own sermons or a reformer who does not want to be reformed himself.

I was once dealing with a difficult parish situation, where people were at loggerheads with one another. I rather fancied myself as a spiritual guide on that occasion, telling them things which it was helpful for them to hear, and doing them a lot of good. On that same evening in church I found myself kneeling next to one of the few men whom I actively dislike, a dislike which was not at that time under control. It was a moment of truth, when I saw myself as a spiritual fraud.

What does this insincerity look like from God's point of view? The prospect is alarming for we know that he cares intensely about the moral law. The Lord is our friend and our brother, but not in the sense of being a pal who turns a blind eye towards our irregularities. He is not 'such a one as we are'.

The two charges, of failure on both the vertical and the horizontal planes, are so patently true that all we can do is to hang our heads in shame and plead guilty. Yet the verdict and the sentence are never given. Instead the final section of the psalm contains a warning and a promise.

The warning is about forgetting God. There are many things which are easy to forget – people's names, what happened yesterday, promises that we have made – but how is it possible to forget God? It happens only when we push him away from the central concerns of our life to its margins, and the best way to bring him back to the centre is to start with thanksgiving which is good, and go on to what Matthew Henry called 'thanksliving' which is better.

The promise is that, if we honour him with our worship and obey him in our lives, we shall know him as our saviour. But we should put that the other way round – if we come to him as our saviour, he will enable us to honour him in our worship and to obey him in our lives.

Thus out of the compost heap, out of the dead and rotting matter, comes the possibility of conversion. The judgement upon our sins, our failures, and the wasted parts of our existence does not in itself bring renewal, but it makes it possible for God, out of the revolting mess, to create new life.

17 HAVE MERCY (51)

When we have wanted to think about our sins the traditional psalm for us to turn to has been 51, but before we do that now we should be clear that this psalmist is more interested in God's forgiveness and renewal than he is in our failures. It is the divine fact of God's generous love which should guide us in all our thinking about our lapses. This is understood by the writer of this psalm, whose main concern is communion with God to which sin is the great obstacle.

He has accepted responsibility for his sin, and so he begins with a prayer for cleansing. 'I acknowledge my faults and my sin is ever before me.' He is a man of such honesty that it does not occur to him to set on the other side of the balance sheet any good things he has done or any temptations he has overcome. One of my staff was accused of rudeness and, when I confronted him with this, he said: 'If I was rude I am sorry, but I didn't intend to be rude.' Here was a double qualification; perhaps he was not rude after all or, if he was, the fact that he didn't mean to be apparently put everything right. I should have been happier if he had said: 'I was rude, and I am sorry.'

Today many Christians tell us that it is neurotic to allow more than a passing glance at our sins. God is our Father and he loves us, and thinking much about sin simply shows how bad we really are. I suspect that this is one more dodge for getting out of self-examination. We should ask for courage to see ourselves as realistically as this psalm does, pulling the wool neither over our own eyes nor over God's eyes. We need 'truth in the inward parts', in those areas of our life which are known to God alone.

Most of our sins are against others and so, in addition to asking God's forgiveness, we should also confess to the neighbour whom we have wronged; and this may be harder than confessing to God. Sometimes we cannot do this and then we must leave the matter in God's hands, as happened to the young man who said: 'As a teenager I treated my mother abominably, and I always intended to make it up to her later, but now she is dead and I can't do a thing about it.' In addition to confessing to others, we must also try to forgive others for the wrong they have done to us, for Jesus said: 'If you do not forgive men their trespasses, neither will your Father forgive your trespasses.' But if the other person is not penitent we cannot completely forgive him, since that means restoring him to friendship with us. What we can do is what Christ did from the cross – pray for his forgiveness, and have such a forgiving and sensitive attitude towards him that it will be easy for him to ask our forgiveness when he is ready to do so.

The psalm goes on to an act of confidence that God will cleanse us. Because he is God, he not only calls us to account and makes demands upon us and brings us to judgement; he reveals his grace in that judgement by having a plan to renew us.

For cleansing is not enough. Inward renewal is also needed, and this can come about only through God's power. He alone provides us with a new and steadfast spirit which will keep us unmoved by temptation. Self-conquest is a dream word, for only God can give us the new heart. The great verses of the psalm are those at the centre: 'Make me a clean heart, O God, and renew a right spirit within me. Cast me not away from thy presence, and take not thy Holy Spirit from me. O give me the comfort of thy help again, and stablish me with thy free spirit.'

In spite of his sins, the psalmist knew that he was in God's presence, and his only fear was that he might be thrown out of it. 'Blessed are the pure in heart', said

Jesus, 'for they shall see God.' When God has completed the process of cleansing us, we shall not only be in his presence; we shall have the greater blessing of knowing that we are in his presence, for we shall see him.

The last thoughts in the psalm concern the resolutions that we should make in thanksgiving for our cleansing. First we are to be on mission, to convert sinners, and to teach God's ways to those who do not know him. Instead of valuing our forgiveness in such a way that we want to hug it to ourselves as our own secret treasure, we should share it with others by drawing them into the orbit of that divine forgiveness.

Secondly we are to adore God and to sing his praises. God will 'open our lips and our mouth will show forth his praise'. For praise is a gift from God and is meaningless unless God has opened our lips to praise him, though it is a gift which we have to use.

Thirdly we are to live a life of self-sacrifice. 'The sacrifice of God is a broken spirit' – not a troubled spirit as the prayerbook has it since, once we are forgiven, our hearts are not troubled – for the obstinacy of pride must be broken and replaced by a life of humility and self-denial, a life of dying to our self-importance and our self-will.

The last two verses are an anti-climax and should perhaps be cut out or treated as an appendix. After these great spiritual depths we end up by building walls and offering young bullocks on the altar! Yet I suppose that we could interpret them in the light of Calvary, and let them suggest to us the important thought of a sacrifice being offered for us. The animal sacrifices of the temple were useless for the spiritual well-being of men, but the sacrifice of the cross is more than useful. It is essential.

Prayers for Others

18 THE PSALM OF UNITY (133)

This psalm is about *brethren* who dwell together in unity. Here is no starry-eyed idealism concerning the universal brotherhood of man, and the whole world living in love and peace. Our brother is the person who sits next to us in church, who works alongside us, who shares our leisure interests, whose path crosses ours however casually. He is the one whom Jesus calls our neighbour. Sometimes it is right for brethren to part and to go their own ways – for Abraham and Lot, or for the partners in a marriage which has died – but this always means that somewhere there has been a breakdown in love.

It is also about brethren who *dwell* together in unity. Possibly the psalm was written for pilgrims who came from great distances to stay in the holy city at a festival, and who experienced there the joy of living in fellowship. They might in this way have presented only a façade of unity which disappeared as soon as the festival was over. Sometimes after a church service there is a teaparty in the hall where the congregation might appear to an outsider to be a united group. They chat happily – though I have known a punch-up to take place on such an occasion – but then they may go home and forget each other.

Again it is about brethren who dwell together *in unity*. The teaching of Jesus on this subject is startling. He spoke of arriving at the altar with a gift, and there remembering that our brother has something against us. We know that it is wrong to receive communion when we are not 'in love and charity' with our neighbour, but Jesus is talking about an occasion when we feel fine and our conscience is clear, but our wholly unreasonable brother has something against us. It seems as if it is Jesus who is now being unreasonable when he says that we should be reconciled to our brother before we offer our gift to God.

We are not always reconciled very fast with our brother, but when it does happen – when disciples are united in prayer and life – it is a good and joyful thing, for it is here that God bestows his blessing, which is life for evermore. Or perhaps we should put that the other way round and say that it is only when God bestows his blessing that such unity becomes possible. For in the words of an old hymn:

Blest be the tie that binds
Our hearts in mutual love.
The fellowship of kindred minds
Is like to that above.

This psalm illustrates the beauty of unity in two ways. First it is said to be like the anointing oil that was poured freely over the head of the high priest, and that ran down over his beard and clothes. This sounds strange because, when the holy oil is used today, it is in minute quantities which are scarcely visible on the forehead. Confirmation candidates, for instance, would not be enchanted if a jug of oil was poured over their heads on to their white dresses and new suits. When I was a recent convert to the Anglican Church, I remember the embarrassment which this verse caused me. What would my pagan friends think if they heard me singing this sort of thing? Of course there is nothing odd about beards, because we have all had to relearn the faces of our friends who have grown beards; and we know also about aftershave lotion, which is poured expensively over the male face, and which now appears to be no longer a luxury, but one of the necessities of living.

Perhaps it is best to forget about Aaron and his beard and to think instead of a woman who took an alabaster box of very expensive perfumed oil, and poured it over the head of Jesus – and she wasn't fussy about what it did to his suit. So the spirit of Christian brotherhood flows in glory from the head, who is Christ, down upon the believers. 'I do not pray for these only', Jesus said, 'but also for those who believe in me through their word, that they may all be one.' This illustration tells us that the spirit of unity is costly and lavish and fragrant.

The beauty of unity is also said to be like dew, which can be a main source of life in a dry land. On the Makonde plateau in my first diocese in southern Tanzania, the rainfall is minimal but heavy dew makes even a good rice crop possible. In the morning it often looks as if it had been raining and, before water had been pumped up a thousand feet, people took their morning bath by rolling in the dewy grass. Even now some older men resent paying a cent or two for tap water, and prefer to send their women down the escarpment to bring up free water in pots on their heads. They say that, apart from drinking water, the dew is good enough, and in any case the daily walk to the well keeps the women out of mischief. So this illustration tells us that the spirit of unity is refreshing and life-giving and gentle and – again – that it flows down from above, from Christ himself.

Unity should be the theme song of our lives as Christians. There must be unity in our own hearts, for sometimes we are so full of temptations and tensions and conflicting aims that there seem to be six people inside us instead of one. This unity also can come only from above, from Christ himself.

Then there must be unity with others. In Christian circles unity today has become a code word for uniting the churches. Certainly we must pray and work for this, but there are other kinds of unity. If we can reconcile young and old, we shall have gone deep into unity. Reconciliation between black and white in South Africa seems a long way off, but there are some hopeful signs and if God is with us we can never lose hope. Unity between conservative and radical is perhaps the greatest need of all – between those who are opposed to change and those who desire change.

The temptation is to say that these are vast issues far beyond the control of ordinary people like ourselves. But in fact we can all do something, even if it is only giving time to understand and love someone of another church, another age group, another colour, another point of view. Unity with others does not just happen. It has to be worked for and prayed for and learned the hard way. It is costly because it means trying to find out what makes the other person tick; it means admitting that we might be wrong; it means a willingness to leave entrenched positions in which we are comfortably settled.

Some verses by Karle Baker picture the Lord as a schoolmaster teaching his class the difference between the singular 'I' and the plural 'We':

'The Lord said,
  "Say, 'We' ";
  But I shook my head,
  Hid my hands tight behind my back, and said,
  Stubbornly,
  "I".

'The Lord said,
  "Say, 'We' ";
  But I looked upon them, grimy, and all awry.
  Myself in all those twisted shapes? Ah, no!
  Distastefully I turned my head away,
  Persisting,
  "They".

'The Lord said,
  "Say, 'We' ";
  And I
  At last
  Richer by a hoard

Of years
And tears,
Looked in their eyes and formed the heavy word
That bent my back and lowed my head:
Like a shamed schoolboy then I mumbled low,
"We,
Lord".'

Above all we must be united with Christ and let his unity flow down into us. Only then shall we be able to live as a unity within ourselves and in unity with our brethren. We have been given vast resources for this in the sacraments, the Bible, prayer, the Christian community. In so far as we live in Christ, we shall live in unity with others.

19 HUMILITY (131)

I wonder whether I can honestly pray this psalm because I know that sometimes at least I am high-minded, high-handed, highbrow, and highsounding, that I do have proud looks, and indeed proud thoughts and a proud heart too. Purple traditionally is the bishop's colour, but we are tending to give it up nowadays because there is an embarrassingly large number of other words which also begin with the letter 'p' – prelacy, pomposity, pride, pretentiousness, presumption, to name only a few. Although we do not change ourselves by changing our dress, at least we have been warned.

Moreover, when the psalm says: 'I do not exercise myself in great matters which are too high for me', I have often wished that I did not have to tackle problems whose solution was beyond me, but my duty compelled me to try. And as for the matters of faith and the purposes of God, they are indeed great matters and too high for us, and yet we have to exercise ourselves in them.

The psalm must therefore be thought of as a prayer that we might become more humble, refrain our soul, and become as a child, trusting in the Lord and not caring about what others think but only about what he thinks – from this time forth (starting not tomorrow but at this very minute) and for evermore (never letting up until pride has been overcome).

The illustration of the weaned child is interesting. A small baby which feeds at his mother's breast is demanding and complains if his demands are not satisfied, but when he is weaned from breast feeding to hand feeding and then to self feeding, he decreases his selfish demands and simply enjoys being with his mother, loving her for what she is and not only for what she gives him. Similarly we Christians in our moods of pride demand from God things for ourselves but if we are able to restrain our ambition and become calmly content to accept God's will for us, we shall attain an inner poise, a repose of soul, an untroubled heart. Self-discipline has a place in achieving this, but mainly it comes from letting God control us at the centre of our life.

Ambition is wrong not in itself but only when it is an expression of self-interest. It is often a powerful motive for the achievement of good, and certainly we should be spiritually ambitious for, unless we aim high in prayer, faith, and witness to Christ, we shall remain spiritual mediocrities. The Bible has much to say about humility, but this is a challenge to be realistic and to see ourselves as we are. If God has given us an important role in life, we must accept that gladly, but we must not boast about it as if we had got there by our own efforts. If he has given us an unimportant role, we must accept that gladly too, instead of living in a dream world where we imagine ourselves to be greater than we are. If God wants us to do great things for him and we shrink from them into a quiet corner, that is false humility, and we should be ashamed of it.

It is only when we – whether individually or as a Church – *trust in the Lord* that God enables us to see ourselves as he sees us; and so we grow into the beautiful virtue of humility and other people find it easier to live with us.

20 PATIENCE (40)

Not surprisingly this psalm is said on Good Friday, for there is much in it that speaks to us of Christ. It interprets sacrifice in terms of obedience – lo I come to do thy will – as the response of the ideal servant. When Christ gave himself totally for us, he 'did not keep back God's loving mercy and truth' from us.

The psalm begins: 'I waited patiently'. Even when the writer was about to sink into the horrible pit, into the mire and clay of sin and death and hell, before he was snatched back, he waited patiently. Yet in spite of this admirable patience, we find him subsequently demanding – in words that have become familiar as the opening phrases of Morning and Evening Prayer – that God should make haste to help him. And the psalm ends with: 'Make no long tarrying, O my God'. This reminds us of Daniel's prayer: 'O Lord, give heed and act! Delay not!'

This is a clear expression of one of the commonest and most painful of Christian tensions. We possess faith – and yet we have to strive for faith. In our worship and preaching we proclaim Christ's triumphant victory – but in our need and weakness it sometimes looks as if the world had been unaffected by Christ's coming. We have Christ – and yet we are waiting for him. We possess the Spirit – and yet we say: Come Holy Ghost.

In asking God to hurry up, the psalmist is speaking, not in dignified liturgical cadences, but out of a real situation. When we are in trouble the first thing, though by no means the only thing, is to shout: Help! After the election of a Superior one of the nuns said: 'We have been praying throughout the night, and this morning we are all taking tablets because our heads ache.' It is right that prayer should begin by asking God urgently to get a move on, but it should not end until there is the peace of acceptance.

For God rarely seems to heed our advice that he should hurry up. The Japanese theologian Kosume Koyama asks what is the use to us in this supersonic age of a God who has always moved at the pace of an oxwaggon. It took him forty years to get his people from Egypt to Israel, and even all that crowd could be airlifted now in two or three days. It took him a thousand years – of judges, kings, prophets, exile, wars – to make the world ready for the coming of his Son. The Son took thirty years to grow up at Nazareth, and the only thing we know about this period is that he *stayed behind* in Jerusalem. Finally, when history had reached what looked like its climax, and God could have been expected to act with lightning speed, nothing happened at all, for there he was at Calvary, nailed to a cross and completely immobile.

If it comes to that, it has taken him another two thousand years to get from Calvary to the present day, and some say that he has not achieved much in that long time either. We know that many blessings have been brought to the world by the Christian religion – the inspiration of dedicated lives, concern for the poor and downtrodden, the glory of Christian culture, to name only a few – but violence, hatred, and selfishness remain. And indeed we ourselves have existed on the earth for a number of years and are still a long way from being perfect. Again we pray for the recovery of a loved one, or the coming home again of a prodigal child, or our own return to an untroubled mind; and it may take God ages to answer, if he answers at all.

Why doesn't God hurry up? We glance at our watches, complain that he is late, and, unable to wait any longer, get on with our own plans in our own way. We work out God's schedule for him and decide what he ought to be doing in the world, and the date by which he ought to have done it. It seems as if he was admirably suitable for previous ages when history flowed slowly, but we have rushed on now and left him behind, and we wonder whether we do not need a new saviour for the new jet age.

We want God to hurry up. But at this point we had better be silent and listen to what he has to say about it all. He is at the centre of all things, and it is not for us to draw up his programme. When a distinguished visitor comes to us from overseas, we are wise to ask him what he would like to do and what he is prepared to do. Otherwise the schedule which we draw up may have to be altered radically, and the result will be confusion. So this psalm says to God: 'Great are the wondrous works which thou hast done . . . and there is no man that ordereth them unto thee.'

Fortunately God refuses to give us up. 'The Lord careth – takes thought for – me', and this gives me great assurance. In the end he always gets without fail to the place which he wants to reach. So instead of criticizing him for not going faster, we had better slow down and adjust ourselves to his pace. We have made a cult of speed and it is producing for us a violent and impersonal society in which we are forgetting what it means to be human.

God knows what he is doing and 'he that keepeth thee will neither slumber nor sleep'. If he hurries, he hurries slowly. His method, as Isaiah said, is 'precept upon precept, precept upon precept, line upon line, line upon line, here a little, there a little'.

Some of the Lord's followers were anxious to bring in the kingdom of heaven immediately, but Jesus was not. Others were discouraged because many things were wrong with the Church, but Jesus was not. After the resurrection many Christians felt frustrated because the end of the world had not occurred, but Jesus taught us through his apostles to go on faithfully, whether the world is to end tomorrow or long after we are dead. What we have to do, then, is to run *with patience* the race that is set before us and wait until God is ready to act. Habbakuk said: 'If the vision delays, wait for it. At the destined hour it will come.' This is also one of the great messages of the psalter as a whole to our modern world: Wait for it!

We have all had experience of waiting – for holidays or retirement, for someone to keep an appointment or to get out of a job so that we could get in, for our first pay cheque or our first car. But what is important is the spirit in which we wait, especially when we are waiting for God. The old Latin title of this psalm is: *Expectans expectavi* – I have waited waitingly – but we often wait only because we have to do so, and very impatiently.

They that wait upon the Lord, as Isaiah said, shall renew their strength, and this means that true patience is creative. It is more than putting up with things and keeping quiet until they improve, and it is the opposite of idleness for it is the using of a time for waiting to prepare for what is coming, and so to grow in faith. Jesus said that we are to be like men who wait for their master's return from a party, and who are ready to let him in the moment he knocks at the door; and almost his last words before his ascension were: Wait for the promise of the Spirit. When the Master has come and the Spirit has been given, we shall know more about the speed with which God acts.

21 CHRIST'S PASSION (22)

We could ask who wrote this psalm and in what circumstances; we could ask what it means to us now; but here I ask instead what it meant for Christ on the cross – not making a psychological inquiry into what he was experiencing there, but seeing how much light this psalm can throw on the passion. For when he said: 'My God, my God, why hast thou forsaken me?', I assume that he was not only quoting the first line of this psalm but praying the whole of it and identifying himself with it. Much of it is applied to Christ in the New Testament, almost all of it could be applied to him, and some of it can be applied to no one else.

We see him at Calvary overwhelmed by a poignant loneliness, for God has hidden himself and left him on his own. The desolation was not complete, for despite his complaints he found some comfort, but in the punch-up that was going on in his soul between belief and despair, the despair seemed predominant. He was sure that God existed, yet, in his utter humiliation and with the whole world against him, it was hard for him to believe.

Looking at this in more detail, we find him asking why God has forsaken him, and why he is so far from his health, which means so far from saving him. We want to say: Of course he needed no salvation and he never was actually forsaken by his Father; he only imagined it, he only felt like that, and this just shows how dangerous it is to trust your feelings. It cannot have happened because the Father and the Son are eternal and inseparable.

That is true as far as it goes, but we cannot get away from Paul's startling words: Christ committed no sin, and yet for our sake *God made him to be sin.* Somehow in a way beyond the range of explanation Jesus identified himself with us sinners and our sin. To this extent he *was* abandoned and rejected by his Father, for this is what sin inevitably does – it separates us from God – and so there is a sense in which the saviour needed to be saved.

He cried in the night season, taking no rest in Gethsemane, and in the daytime on the cross. But the prayer book translation is wrong in saying that God did not hear him. He heard him all right but he did not answer. The distinction is important, for a God who does not hear is a remote, uninvolved God; but a God who does not answer may have the most loving reason for not doing so.

In spite of some hopeful considerations he felt that he was no better than a worm. Despised, defenceless, no longer treated as a human being – the black people of South Africa know what this means – he needed the encouragement that Isaiah gave: 'Fear not, Jacob, you worm, and Israel, you poor louse.'

The laughter, the scorn, the blasphemous attack on his faith are so true of what happened at Calvary that many commentators suppose that the passion narrative has been influenced by this psalm. The old tradition saw it as a foretelling of certain things that would happen. 'The prophets', said Peter, 'foretold the sufferings in store for Christ.' When John so closely reflects the later verse about parting his garments and casting lots for his vesture, was he writing history or was he writing theology? Moltmann makes an important point when he tells us that we should let Calvary show us what this psalm means, rather than letting the psalm show us what Calvary means. We should be making a great mistake if we supposed that Christ had to fit his passion into the pattern laid down by this psalm, or again to imagine that this psalm can explain to us adequately the meaning of the cross. It can, however, illuminate what happened at Calvary, and it is itself illuminated and given new depths of meaning by what happened at Calvary; for Jesus was talking about 'my

God' – the God to whom he was so close, and not to the Covenant God of the Old Testament – and he was crying out not in self-pity, but because he wanted God's faithfulness to be vindicated.

The reference to his mother's womb switches our thoughts to the manger at Bethlehem and the childhood at Nazareth, but we are not allowed to stay there long, for trouble was near and there was no helper. Jesus trod the winepress alone, for his disciples had forsaken him.

The fat bulls of Bashan closed in upon him, and the death-powers of this bullring treated him as a blasphemer, sabbath-breaker, terrorist, and confederate of Satan. He was going downhill and getting weaker but, if the reference to a melting heart means that he had no heart to fight on, this line cannot be applied to Christ. His heart never turned to wax, and he never lost the battle in his soul. The terrible thing about the great sacrifice was that it was God himself who was bringing him into the dust of death.

We are told that they pierced his hands and his feet, but the Hebrew is obscure (NEB has 'they hacked off my hands and my feet'), and this looks like a place where the translators may have allowed the passion narrative to influence the psalm.

Throughout this desolating experience he had been waiting upon God. The tension was between seeking his Father and finding him, and the strain on his faith is reflected in the mounting crescendo of almost unbearable appeal: Be not far from me, Lord! Hasten to help me! Deliver my soul, my darling – which means my life, all I have left – and save me!

We do not know what happened to turn this terrible lament into a song of praise. In the prayer book version the change comes in the middle of a verse, where he is snatched from the lion's mouth, from the very jaws of hell, at the eleventh hour. This dramatic break is not followed in modern versions, though it is supported by conservative commentators such as Kirkpatrick.

In Christ's case we cannot know what happened, and we can only gaze at him in wonder. Did his Father speak to him, flooding his spirit with exultation? Did he recall that the saints of old had never been abandoned? Did he look back over his own experience and see that even in the darkness love always ran on, so that he could say with Job: 'Though he slay me, yet will I trust him'? Did he begin his meditation on this psalm in Gethsemane and if so was it prayer which restored him from uncertainty to confidence? All we know is that, as Weiser says, 'guided by this psalm, he interpreted the way which had led him through his most bitter passion, but ended in the triumph of faith and in the victory of the kingdom of God'.

In the second half of the psalm the triumph comes through loud and clear. Praise is to be given to God, first in Israel, in the church, and Christ was to have a seed, a congregation, of his own. The verse: 'I will declare thy name unto my brethren' is quoted with warm approval by the writer to the Hebrews who hears the Son in this psalm call men his brothers. Naturally this family would include the poor, for they are his special favourites, and he always hears them even though he sometimes hides his face from them. The praise is to culminate in a sacrificial meal, which for most Christians must be the eucharistic feast where the poor eat and are satisfied, for they enjoy eternal life.

Praise is to be given to God secondly in the world. 'All the end of the world shall remember themselves.' Like the prodigal son who 'came to himself', the prodigal nations will turn to the Lord and come into his kingdom and worship him. Here is the epiphany and missionary theme which points to the immense field of opportunity which Calvary has opened up.

Praise is to be given thirdly in the future. There are some obscurities in the text here. The 'fat upon earth' are probably the great ones who are too proud to need God – but they also will have to pay homage to him. 'They that go down into the dust' are probably those in Sheol who also will have to pay homage. The confidence that God's power extends beyond death, and reaches down into hell, is an important step towards the doctrine of resurrection.

Here is a magnificent vision of the triumphant consummation of the kingdom of God which embraces everyone of past, present, and future generations. For 'a people that shall be born' confidently looks forward to a time when God will still be praised here on earth while we are, we trust, praising him in heaven.

As we stand rebuked by this tremendous example of faith and spiritual courage, to which even the greatest of saints cannot come near, the whole of Christ's Church praises him for the completeness of his sacrifice and for his saving death.

22 LIFT UP YOUR HEADS (24)

'Lift up your heads, O ye gates, and be ye lift up, ye everlasting doors: and the king of glory shall come in.' Unless we can see the poetry in these words we shall find them rather ridiculous. How can we talk to a door as if it were a human being? Sometimes I have wanted to say with the psalmist: Hey there, you doors, you are too small! for my two predecessors as bishops of Johannesburg were short men and many church doors in that diocese were made to their measure. When I arrived, wearing a mitre and standing seven feet from the ground, I sometimes had to stoop before I could enter a church. The psalmist, then, is saying to the doors of the temple: 'Do you want the great king to get down on his hands and knees and *crawl* through you? Then stretch! Make yourselves bigger! Make room for the king of glory to come in!'

We picture a church procession in ancient Jerusalem, consisting of a choir with priests and their attendants, and the head of state and his attendants, going slowly up the hill at the top of which stood the temple. Seeing that its doors were closed, they sang: 'We long greatly to enter; what must we do to have those doors opened for us?'

On the other side of the closed doors another choir, with more priests and their attendants, sang in answer: 'If you want to enter, you must have clean hands and a pure heart.' The procession outside sang back accepting these conditions, the doors were opened, and they went in.

Christians have often applied this psalm to the ascension, and have seen in it Jesus the king of glory coming into his kingdom. He alone is clean of hand and pure of heart, so there is nothing to stop him entering, except that even heavenly doors are too small for his divine majesty. But what about us, the riffraff who are following along with him? There is no reason why the gates of the kingdom should open automatically for us, and our only hope of getting into heaven is that Jesus is taking us there.

A pure heart is not a negative state. In south London it was often said of someone who had died: He never did no harm to nobody. Even if he never did anything worse than illtreat the English language, what a terrible obituary! He never did anything wrong but he never did anything right either. To have a pure heart means more than confessing our sins and accepting God's forgiveness. We also have to learn from God how to worship him, and how to receive from him a spirit of deep amazement, awe, and adoration; for the man with a pure heart lives always in the presence of the holy God. We sing:

> Take my life, and let it be
> Consecrated, Lord, to thee.

But we sometimes change the last word and say: Take my life and let it be consecrated, Lord, to *me*. This is like a small child who gives us a present and almost at once demands it back again. The consecration of self to self brings no joy or satisfaction, and only in so far as we are consecrated to God can we worship him with pure hearts.

During a holiday in Greece I visited a hermitage on a remote corner of the island of Patmos. (It was on this holy island that John the Theologian – the one indisputably political clergyman in the New Testament – wrote the last book of the Bible while he was undergoing there the island arrest which is the equivalent of house arrest in South Africa.) The church was well furnished and spotless, a rowing boat was moored in the bay, there were saltpans on the rocks near the shore, and the garden was a green oasis beneath a bleak hill. The priest, wearing a threadbare cassock, gave me a glass of well water and a piece of turkish delight and, talking through an architectural student from Athens, said that he had lived there for twenty years. He liked to cultivate his farm, and to minister to the handful of people who lived nearby, and to see visitors, but what he liked best of all was to have time to pray. And I thought of certain executives in Johannesburg who drive themselves sick with anxiety, and who do not even suspect that silence has a healing power.

In addition to offering a pure heart in simple devotion to God, we must also have clean hands, which means that we must keep away from what is false, empty, and lacking in integrity, and be true to our neighbour as well as to God. It includes such things as doing an honest day's work, visiting the sick, working for justice and a better social order, and learning how to care for others. Hands which refuse to touch such things become ingrained with selfishness.

We can see how this works out in practice by turning to Paul's splendid summary of the Lord's earthly life in 1 Corinthians 13. By substituting 'Jesus' for 'charity' we find that: 'Jesus is patient and kind . . . Jesus rejoices in the right. Jesus bears all things, believes all things, hopes all things, endures all things'.

But if we cannot do as well as this – if our heart is not as pure as we should like, or our hands particularly clean – we need not be depressed. The psalmist did not know, since he lived before Christ, that God will open the doors of heaven for us anyway. He would prefer us to have pure hearts and clean hands, but he lets us come into his presence as we are – dirty, untidy, travel-stained; and then he gives us the pure hearts and the clean hands for which we have longed.

At the beginning of that letter to Corinth, Paul had spoken in such glowing terms about the Christians there that we expect to find a congregation who are far advanced in sanctity. He thanks God for them, for the grace and enrichment which they have received, for the completeness of their knowledge, and for the fact that they lack no spiritual gift. But we read on and find that the church was notable for disunity, pride, adultery, jealousy, quarrelsomeness, and immaturity. Paul talked as he did because, although he saw the people as they were, he also saw them as Christ wanted them to be – with pure hearts and clean hands. He so identified himself with Christ's caring and sharing that he could go forward confidently to change the actual into the ideal.

This psalm, in singing about the temple doors, has led us to think about heaven's doors, but the same process also works in reverse. God is on the move, and he wants to come into our hearts and take possession of them. If the Most High is to get through these doors, we shall have to unlock them and open them as wide as possible.

In Revelation the church at Laodicea is no more an exemplary church than that at Corinth. We hear them advised to visit their stockbroker, their tailor, and their doctor, so that they might revise their spiritual investments, get some decent clothes to wear, and have a checkup on their souls. Yet Jesus sent this message through John to the Christians in that city: 'I stand at the door and knock; if anyone hears my voice and opens the door, I will come in to him and eat with him, and he with me' (Rev. 3.20). When we complacently suppose that God is already with us in our hearts, we should make sure that he is not all the time outside knocking at the door, and we cannot hear him because there is too much noise inside. But if we open the door, he enters and we have food with him – the sacramental food of the Eucharist, and the spiritual food of scripture and prayer. And so, as certainly as he comes to us here on earth, he will take us through the doors of heaven, that we may be with him for ever.

23 RENEWAL OF THE CHURCH (85)

I call this the 'turning psalm' because the verb 'turn' appears several times in the prayer book version, and indeed in NEB too. God has turned away the captivity that was strangling his Church, he has turned away from his anger, but we still need him to turn us round, if we are to turn to him in penitence. When he turns to us in love we are filled with joy, and his grace stops us from turning away from the right path.

It does not matter whether or not the psalm originally referred to the Babylonian captivity, because we can apply it to any form of captivity which the Church may suffer.

It took me some time to understand the changes of tense. It seemed to be saying: Thank you, God, for turning away your displeasure; now kindly turn it away! There are in fact three scenes, as if in a drama.

The first three verses refer to the past, and to the wonderful things that God has done for his Church. If we are old we can remember some of these things; otherwise we can read about them in the church history books. Past memories should be the subject of continual praise.

The second scene concerns the present, which is felt to be dreadful, and the prayer here is for renewal. Even in its best periods the Church has seen the need to pray for new manifestations of God's power, because life on the frontier of two worlds is never lacking in tensions. In the bad periods we keep going only on hope and prayer – with such prayers as that of Habbakuk: Revive thy work in the midst of the years; or that of the dumb boy's father: Lord I believe, help thou mine unbelief. They also include the prayer of listening. Verse 8 – I will hearken to what the Lord will say – forms the text of the great Book 3 of *The Imitation of Christ.*

With this verse we move into the last scene, which concerns the future. Confidence that salvation is near – that Jesus is near – is brought to the Church by a prophet who can see further ahead than most people; and so this psalm is suitable for Christmastime. We are assured that God is intervening, and bringing a message of hope in the present terrible situation. The whole of this section is really an expansion of the word 'saviour', for Christ alone fulfils this psalm. The triumphal procession is his, and all the others – righteousness, mercy, truth, glory, peace, lovingkindness, prosperity – are his cavalcade of escorts and outriders.

This psalm reminded Matthew Henry of the story of Noah – the first scene looking back to the peaceful life that Noah lived before the deluge came, the second scene representing the appalling experience of being raced away by the floods, and the third the arrival of the dove with an olive-branch which pointed forward to the rainbow and future peace.

It reminds me of Tchaikovsky's ballet of the *Sleeping Beauty*. This begins with a scene of great happiness, resulting from the birth of a lovely child to royal parents who had greatly desired her; and I see in this a picture of the Church whose birth, following the crucifixion and the resurrection, promised the world such wonderful things.

Then the powers of evil came in, and everything went wrong. The growing child, just before coming to the fullness of her beauty, is wounded through the malice of a witch, and it is only the influence of the good fairies which prevents the wound from being fatal. Instead the princess is thrown into a deep sleep, and there she remains for a hundred years. It is not difficult to see the Church as a sleeping beauty; beautiful because God created her, but constantly wounded by the devil and dropping off to sleep. It is all very disappointing, for things have not turned out as we thought that they would, and we have to listen again to the call of the early Christian hymn:

> Awake sleeper, rise from the dead
> And Christ will give you light.

But the Church has no power of its own to wake up, and we have to wait for God – who, in spite of what some other psalms say about him, neither slumbers nor sleeps – to awake us with his kiss of life. It is God who prevents the wound – the bruise inflicted by the serpent – from being fatal, and it is God who restores his Church to mobility again. So there is joy beyond description, Puss in Boots and Red Riding Hood in the ballet and mercy, righteousness, and the others here, joining together to dance the happy ending which is also the beginning of a new life.

Like the Church, we as individuals have received enormous privileges of body, mind, and soul – to be alive and well, to have security, culture, wealth, vocation, friends. But these are transient because, even if today we enjoy all these privileges – and many people never enjoy some of them – tomorrow our health might collapse, our country be plunged into revolution, our friends die. The present becomes more bleak as we realize that there are certain privileges which we ought to give up, as Christ gave us his when he moved towards Calvary; and if any privilege prevents us from freely making decisions for Christ we should abandon it. There cannot, however, be any doubt about the future. When we come at last to the beatific vision there will be privileges beyond our dreams or imagination; and this thought gives us confidence to go on through the dark days.

24 THE DEVOUT LIFE (1)

The first psalm is an aperitif before a meal, a trailer for a forthcoming film, a waiting room outside a great man's office, and it tells us what we are to look for in the rest of the psalter. It starts with a beatitude: 'Blessed is the man' – the devout man. He is like a tree, perhaps in that semi-tropical setting an evergreen date palm, transplanted to a watered garden such as that spoken of in Ecclesiastes: 'I made myself gardens and parks, and planted in them all kinds of fruit trees. I made myself pools from which to water the forest of growing trees.' The tree draws up the grace of God through its roots, and this is the source of the devout man's happiness.

In the divine biology these people are recognized, as Jesus said, by their fruits. I think of an invalid woman afflicted with a dozen diseases and frailties, whose faith made it a refreshment to visit her; of a greathearted pastor who helped me more than ever he knew; of the Salvation Army officers who attended a High Mass to find out what it was that made one of their clerks such a fine Christian. As we pray for such people we can thank God, with Jeremiah, that their soul is a 'watered garden'.

The psalmist is not, however, helpful when he gives as a motive for leading the devout life – the promise that those who obey God will be successful, whereas the wicked will be carried off like the wind, and lost like worthless chaff. Most people have at one time or another tried to drive a bargain with God on these lines. 'If you will get me through the examination I will lead a good life.' Often this does not work in fact, and in any case our better selves tell us that we should do what is right for the love of God alone, and not for what we are going to get out of it. Yet on the other hand faith believes that the life of the wicked, though temporarily successful, will be seen to be a failure on the day of judgement, whereas nothing that is done in accordance with the will of God can ultimately fail.

The fact is that this writer is an 'either – or' man. In the last verse he sees a straight choice between two ways. (Did this give the Lord the idea for his teaching about the two roads?) The road forks, and one path leads directly to God, but the other is a desert trail which peters out at a dried-up waterhole around which lie the skeletons of travellers who took the wrong road. Whether or not the distinction is as clear as this psalm makes out, sooner or later we have to make the decision between the devout life and the worldly life.

One of the marks of the devout life is self-denial. Christianity has often been criticized for being negative, and it is sad if negation controls our religious outlook; but we cannot advance along the right road without sometimes saying No. In the first verse we have a progression of negatives. Blessed is the man who does not *walk in* – is not influenced by – the ways of the *worldly*: who does not *stand* – actually share in – the practices of *sinful* men: who does not *sit* – identify himself completely with – the mockers, those who used quaintly to be called 'freethinkers', who smile at the idea of God, and who corrupt the young by denying moral values.

The right kind of self-denial makes progress possible, and so is positive. It is like an expert gardener who tells me to stop pruning my roses in the way that I am doing and to prune them in another way so that they will grow better. God asks us to give up things, not because that is commendable in itself, but in order to help us grow. We are followers of one who told us to deny ourselves, take up our cross and follow him; and we should find out what are the things in our life against which we put up a No Entry notice, and then ask whether in fact we have put the notice on the right doors.

Another mark of the devout man is obedience, and that is not a popular word either; but this psalm calls us to responsible obedience, to follow law and not legalism – are we sure that we know the difference in our own lives? – and so find great joy. 'His delight is in the law of the Lord.' That was the shape of obedience as we see it in the life of the incarnate Lord, for he said that it was food and drink for him to do his Father's will. The law that he came to obey is not the law that Paul found irksome, but the divine law of love.

Jesus alone fulfils the psalmist's conception of perfect obedience but, although we are disobedient, he makes it possible for us to move towards his perfection. He does this through his cross, which the old commentators thought was referred to in the tree by the waterside.

When we consider the place of obedience in our own lives, rules should be kept to a minimum and should aim only at strengthening weak points. For example, if we want to pray but never seem able to get down to it, we should do well to bind ourselves to pray at certain times and for a specified length of time. Or if we have some particular difficulty about relating to other people – we are too diffident or withdrawn, or too impatient and aggressive – we could try to make a rule about that.

But when we make rules we had better see that they are practical, for in prayer time it is easy to plant both feet firmly in mid-air and to say, for instance: 'From now onwards I resolve always to love my neightbour as myself.' It would be preferable to say: 'From now onwards I will fight against my jealousy of that particular person.' In the Lord's parable of the Two Sons, the one who said: 'I go, sir', but did not go, scored no marks at all. Nor must we try to do a whole lot of things that we cannot do in our own strength. Rather we must trust in God, the all loving and the all powerful, in whose obedient service we shall find our freedom.

25 PRAYER FOR COMMITTED CHRISTIANS (16)

This is a psalm we can pray for anyone who sincerely wishes to commit his life to God. 'Preserve me', it begins – preserve us from the daily temptations and sins which make it difficult to live the life of dedication. The psalmist says: 'Thou are my God.' He has made the great decision to give his life to God, and no doubt it is God himself who is the origin of this decision for the initiative is always in his hands. He chooses us and calls us to follow him.

A young priest, able and hardworking, committed himself to the Church as a career, with indeed considerable loss of worldly prospects, but he knew little of personal devotion to God, and this became clear at a point of moral crisis. But instead of seeing the faults of another it would be better to look into our own hearts and ask ourselves: Have I made the decision to give my life to God? And if I have, do I not need constantly to renew that decision?

The psalmist sees before him a straight choice between life with God and life without God. He spells this out negatively by saying that he will not allow his religion to be contaminated by external influences. We criticized early missionaries to Africa who identified the gospel message with western music, architecture, and clothes, but we are less quick to criticize our own identification of the gospel with worldly attitudes.

No doubt there has been some element of trust in God for as long as there has been any personal religion among men, but it was Isaiah who first gave this trust a central place ('in quietness and in confidence shall be your strength'), and here we are called to trust God all the way, knowing that he is showing us 'the path of life', and that he is leading us onwards into fellowship with him. It does not mean that if we trust God everything will turn out to be smooth and easy for us, but rather it is a letting go, a letting God take over and then cheerfully walking along the path of life, which is often rough and difficult.

The psalm, then, is a song of confidence. 'The lot is fallen unto me in a fair ground; yea I have a goodly heritage.' What does this mean to a black man in a white dominated society, or to a bourgeois in a country where power is passing into the hands of socialists? Are we confident that God has given us a wonderful place in a wonderful Church, and do we enjoy our religion and give ourselves gratefully to it? (If we do we shall also be compelled to work towards a fairer ground and a better heritage for those who are less privileged.) Or are we as Christians involved in a crisis of identity, and do we feel frustrated, inadequate failures, in spite of the fact that God is 'the portion of our inheritance'? Or again perhaps we feel: It is all very well to have the Lord as my portion – the place where I live and work – but I would like a portion of visible success and encouragement as well! Whenever we experience doubt or despair, this psalm recalls us to a joyful confidence.

Peter quoted verse 11, saying that the psalmist here 'spoke with foreknowledge of the resurrection of the Messiah'. In fact 'the holy one' refers to each of us, for God promises that he will not leave us in hell. Peter's mistake was, however, a fortunate one for it justifies us in reading into the psalm something that was not in the writer's mind – the resurrection of Christ. He who is risen is with us and gives us a share in his resurrection life; and this is a greater ground for confidence than anything the psalmist knew.

Verses 8-10 reveal a deep awareness of the presence of God who goes before us as a guide and who is at our right hand as a companion. This is allied to the thought of the last verse where the known presence of God brings the fullness of joy. The 'night season' refers to those secret, silent, solitary disciplines of prayer, at whatever hour they take place, when we commune with God and receive his chastening instruction. The reference to 'my cup' surely suggests to us the eucharistic chalice, the cup that satisfies all our thirst, for in the Eucharist there is prayer in its perfection.

The prayer book version of verse 3 reads: 'All my delight is upon the saints that are in the earth', and if this is the correct reading it reminds us that we have to delight in the saints even when they are far from being saintly. We have to be concerned about the people for whom Christ died, and we should do this gladly, not in a spirit of restraint or even of duty, for we should *delight* in them. However, the Hebrew is obscure, and many scholars think that we should read with NEB: 'The gods whom earth holds sacred are all worthless, and cursed are all who make them their delight'. Such gods as false ideologies, money, or power are a continuing threat because, worthless though they truly are, they are popularly thought to be of great worth. But at the end of the day they will bring only disaster to those who delight in them.

But if it is the saints in whom we delight, we must thank the Lord for giving us warning, or counsel — that inspired understanding which enables us to relate to others as we should. Compassion has to be combined with wisdom, for it is possible to get so emotionally involved with the problems of others that we not only wear ourselves out, but in the long run fail to help others as we should, since we have ceased to be objective. Detachment is needed, yet detachment can turn into a clinical interest which says and does the right things but fails to treat people as people.

We do not get far with trying to 'delight in the saints' without finding how easy it is to hurt others and to be hurt by them. Neville Ward says that, because we have not the power to hurt on a large scale, we hurt and get hurt in small areas, and the smaller the area the greater the hurt. This occurs especially in the intimacy of the family. I know that, as a teenager, I often hurt my father. A wife said: 'I can't tell my husband that he has hurt me, because he is a dominant personality who will at once produce three reasons why I ought not to have been hurt.' In another family the husband is a man of routine, but his wife is generally late with the breakfast and his shirts are rarely ironed on time; so they continually hurt each other.

When we are hurt, the answer is not to sulk and draw attention to ourselves, or to grit our teeth and put up with it stoically, or to work it off in hatred against someone else, or to nurse our bitterness secretly until it becomes a permanent scar. The Lord accepted hatred, and he was hurt more seriously than we shall ever be, yet he never ceased to forgive and pray for those who wronged him.

Only the counsel that God gives, only a commitment to him so deep that its issue is complete confidence in him, only a life of prayer which is also a life of love for others, can provide us with the right balance here.

26 PRAYING FOR OUR COUNTRY (72)

This is a coronation psalm telling us of the good time expected during the new reign. If it is intended to be a prophecy it is ludicrous, for no government anywhere in the world – let alone that of Solomon if it was originally spoken for him – has ever come near to achieving the justice, peace, prosperity, and freedom which are foretold here. As a prophecy it can be applied only to the kingdom of Christ, through whom alone integrity, universal rule, and the other blessings will come to all the world. That is why it has become an epiphany psalm.

Apart from this, the best way to use it is as a prayer for the government of whatever country we live in.[1] When we pass judgement on our government there should be an element of penitence in judgement since the government is not an entity different from ourselves. There should also be a readiness to recognize, even if we are convinced supporters of the opposition, that some of the things done by our government are good. We pray, therefore, not primarily for a political party, but for the realm itself and for its appointed leaders, for the backroom boys in the civil service, for the police, for the magistrates, and for all who influence public opinion. If we pray from the heart and not only in words, our prayer will issue in action, and our opponents will accuse us of mixing religion with politics; but if the prayer is right, we can leave that issue in the hands of God.

In such prayer we should aim high, praying that God will grant our country as many of his perfect gifts as we are capable of receiving. The psalm makes clear that the first thing to be prayed for – before ever we get on to

[1] In v.15 'prayer shall be made ever unto him' should read 'prayer shall be made for him'. This has been corrected in most modern versions.

power or peace or prosperity – is justice. The basic petition is : Enable my government to support the weak who lack support – to provide education, medical aid, and social security for those who cannot provide these things for themselves; to end the oppression that makes the havenots victims of the haves; to see that social responsibility is the main plank in our national policy. God alone is the source of that justice by which the life of the community is sustained, and we pray that our rulers may understand this.

We should pray that our government may be strong; it must be so if it is to 'defend the children of the poor and punish the wrongdoer', and if it is to secure peace as well as justice for its people. Surely we are right to pray also that our country may be prosperous, that its corn and fruit may abound, provided that this prosperity is shared and not made the privileged possession of a minority. The prayer here is that nature may find such harmony with man that the land itself may happily contribute to peace and righteousness. This is more than a poetic fancy, for where a government is fully responsible there will be an enlightened agricultural policy which will include tree planting and the combating of erosion and pollution, and which will promote the right development of natural resources.

The thought of dominion 'from one sea to the other' might in past centuries have suggested a single power exercising control over the world. Perhaps it still does this to China and Russia, but now we are beginning to understand that true patriotism looks beyond itself, and what we have to pray for is that the United Nations may be so radically transformed that the nations could gladly give it their support, knowing that moral supremacy is the only supremacy that matters, and that the only true victory is moral victory. We have to pray also that even 'the dwellers in the wilderness' – the wild untouchable

Bedouin, the most extreme of atheistic communists – may kneel before God as their Father and live peacefully with their brothers.

So we come to the blessing with which the psalm ends, and which we can interpret as a beatitude. Happy are those who refer the whole of their political life and all its decisions to the Lord God for his guidance, since what we desire above all is that the earth should be filled with his glory.

God, you only can make leaders into good leaders,
Give our rulers wise and understanding hearts
That, animated by your spirit of justice,
They may hear the cry of the oppressed,
And find their glory in redressing human wrongs
And in securing peace and plenty for your people.

Father, give to our rulers the knowledge of what is right,
And power to get the right done.
May they know that all authority is yours,
That they are responsible to you for exercising it,
And that they must give to you an account of their
stewardship.

BIBLIOGRAPHY

Commentaries to which I am indebted

Eaton, J. H., *Psalms*. Torch Bible Commentaries. SCM Press 1967.

Hargreaves, John, *A Guide to Psalms*. TEF Study Guide 6. SPCK 1973.

Henry, Matthew, *Commentary on the Whole Bible*. The most convenient format is that edited by Leslie Church, published by Marshall, Morgan & Scott 1961.

Hill, Edmund, *Prayer, Praise and Politics*. Sheed & Ward 1973.

Lewis, C. S., *Reflections on the Psalms*. Collins Fontana 1958.

Palmer, R. F., *Psalms Then and Now*. Canada, SSJE Bracebridge, 1965.

Slack, Kenneth, *New Light on Old Songs*. SCM Press 1975.

Weiser, Artur, *The Psalms*, Old Testament Library. SCM Press 1962.

Modern versions of the text

The Common Bible (the ecumenical edition of the Revised Standard Version). Collins Fontana.

The Jerusalem Bible. Darton, Longman & Todd.

The New English Bible (NEB). OUP and CUP.

Baughen, M.A., ed., *Psalm Praise*. Falcon Books 1973.

Gelineau, Joseph, *The Psalms: A New Translation*. Collins Fontana 1972.

The Psalms in Today's English Version (TEV). Collins Fontana 1972.

The Revised Psalter. SPCK 1975.

Twenty Five Psalms from a Modern Liturgical Psalter. Church Information Office 1973.

